Frederick C. Kintzer

Foreword by
James L. Wattenbarger

MIDDLEMAN
IN
HIGHER
EDUCATION

 Jossey-Bass Publishers
San Francisco · Washington · London · 1973

LB
2328
K44

MIDDLEMAN IN HIGHER EDUCATION
*Improving Articulation among High School,
Community College, and Senior Institutions*
by Frederick C. Kintzer

Copyright © 1973 by Jossey-Bass, Inc., Publishers

Published and copyrighted in Great Britain by
Jossey-Bass, Ltd., Publishers
3 Henrietta Street
London WC2E 8LU

Copyright under International, Pan American, and
Universal Copyright Conventions. All rights
reserved. No part of this book may be reproduced
in any form—except for brief quotation (not to
exceed 1,000 words) in a review or professional
work—without permission in writing from the publisher.
Address all inquiries to Jossey-Bass Publishers,
San Francisco, California, USA.

Library of Congress Catalogue Card Number LC 72-11969

International Standard Book Number ISBN 0-87589-160-8

Manufactured in the United States of America

JACKET DESIGN BY WILLI BAUM

FIRST EDITION

Code 7303

The Jossey-Bass
Series in Higher Education

JOHN E. ROUECHE, *University of Texas*
Consulting Editor, Community and Junior Colleges

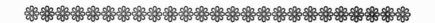

Foreword

When a new community college is established, administrative officers stress to the people living in its service area that the new college's credits will be accepted for transfer. This assurance reflects the natural concern that doors stay open for continued education. As attitudes toward access in higher education have progressed from elitist to meritocratic to egalitarian, the concept of limited access, which was a foundation of most higher education, has been rejected by the public and the educational profession alike. The open door is viewed as a way of equalizing opportunity in life, not just in education. A college education has become a right, not a privilege.

These attitudes provided the basic rationale for the development of community colleges in most states; their growth has been a recognized phenomenon. The total enrollment in higher education —all of it—in 1945 was just equal to the community college enrollment in 1972. Such rapid increase has made higher education much more commonly accepted and considerably more often included in family plans than ever before.

No closed doors, however, means that students who want to continue beyond these egalitarian institutions will be permitted to.

When this continuation is prevented, the student and his parents react with emotion and speed against the community college or the receiving institution or both. Their concern has motivated the passage of laws and other punitive actions designed to correct the problem. Consequently, most community college administrators are actively making arrangements for smooth transfer between the first two years and the last two years of baccalaureate-degree programs. (Unfortunately they do not always show a similar concern for the movement of students from secondary schools to community colleges.)

In the last quarter of this century universal opportunity for continued education during the total lifetime of most individuals will likely become a reality. As more students complete two years of college, more will want to complete four years. But as more people transfer from community colleges to upper divisions, there will be more individual problems to solve.

Solutions to these problems must be found. At one time policy statements unilaterally developed by the receiving institution were the usual answer to transfer problems. These individually oriented policies were often followed by formal agreements which were designed to universalize the individualized solutions. In a few instances, systems of universities handed down policies. In all these cases, however, the community college was placed on the defensive.

By early 1970, in several states, the community colleges were strong enough to require acceptance of their participation in the process through mutual deliberations and decisions. Although this system of reaching agreement has been accepted in only a few states, this process will probably be used more often in the future.

Indications thus are that most college faculty and administrative leadership will be involved in working with students who will attend two or more institutions as they move from freshman through senior years. The problems of articulation then become more nearly a universal concern. *Middleman in Higher Education* provides readers with the background necessary for participation in the process of arriving at solutions to these problems. The perspective of history *Middleman in Higher Education* supplies is particularly helpful, and this book would be noteworthy if that task alone were accomplished.

Frederick Kintzer goes on however to provide examples of procedures used in those states which have studied the problems. These short-cut procedures should be especially useful to those who are just becoming aware of the problems involved. And continued study of these procedures will provide an opportunity for experienced persons to gain perspective on their own problems. *Middleman in Higher Education* thereby becomes an important contribution to the literature of higher education.

Few people have provided more continual analysis of these articulation problems than Kintzer. Few have delved more deeply than he. No one is better prepared to discuss all the ramifications of articulation. Here this problem receives the attention it needs. Hopefully the results will benefit the student.

Gainesville
January 1973

JAMES L. WATTENBARGER
Director
Institute of Higher Education
University of Florida

Preface

As higher education entered the seventies, the flood of high school graduates entering community colleges continued unabated. For the 1970 fall term, community colleges accounted for 41 percent of all freshman enrollment (both baccalaureate degree and non-baccalaureate degree majors) in public higher education systems. In eight states, community colleges enrolled 50 percent or more of all freshmen (National Center for Educational Statistics, 1970).

While national enrollment in community colleges has now generally leveled off and in fall 1971 even declined in a few key states (Lombardi, 1972), the percentage of future enrollment is expected to rise. Several factors lend encouragement to that prediction: lowering of the majority age to eighteen, the increasing numbers of adult students, and the implementation of the Education Amendments Act of 1972, which envisions equal educational opportunities. By the year 2000, community colleges will probably be enrolling from 40 to 45 percent of all undergraduates (Carnegie Commission on Higher Education, 1970b). In view of these enrollment figures, transfer admissions should indeed continue to be big business.

But efforts to make systematic provision for the transfer student have not kept pace with the dramatic increase in numbers of students until recently. At the close of the 1960s, plans for effective transfer were being implemented in only a handful of states and in a scattering of individual institutions. This lag was reported in a monograph on community college state master plans. Hurlburt (1969) analyzed master plans of nineteen states and noted the general lack of information regarding transfer policies and procedures. Articulation was not a statewide matter. Few states were using this effective vehicle to establish priorities where transfer needs were greatest.

As the 1970s began, community colleges remained in a difficult if not untenable position as middlemen in states without systematic plans for effective transfer. Liberal changes in senior college–university admission patterns needed to be supplemented by flexible policies on credit transfer and course acceptance from community colleges. Detailed and cooperative planning was required to assure policy implementation. Transfer admission was rapidly becoming priority business in the educational systems of all but a few states, especially in areas where numbers alone necessitated action. But for the most part policies remained unrefined and unevaluated. All too frequently the fate of the transfer student depended on individual action.

In most states, transfer from junior to senior college is now being given priority. While greatest attention is directed toward the transfer phenomenon in states where two-year colleges are prominent, organized efforts have begun in almost every state to develop transfer guidelines. Often under the aegis of a governmental agency, all segments of higher education within a state are being brought into discussions at an early point, and these discussions are sometimes being continued by task forces—some subject matter–oriented, some oriented toward solving specific problems.

I base these statements on information gathered while completing a nationwide pilot study on articulation published early in 1970 as a topical paper by the ERIC Clearinghouse for Junior Colleges. More than eighty educators in all fifty states contributed to this initial effort to identify tentatively the transfer relationships between two- and four-year colleges. The pilot study was a preliminary investigation for a three-stage research project scheduled for completion by September 1973. Sponsored by the Esso Education Foundation, the project is designed to study the evaluation and application of community college transfer credits and courses by senior colleges and universities in fifty states. The Canadian provinces will also be included in all three stages.

The purposes are to gather and synthesize information in Stage 1 on credit and course relationships in all fifty states; to evaluate articulation models developed in Stage 1; to investigate in Stage 2 student attitudes and report specific transfer problems; to provide bases (Stage 3) for aiding statewide and regional articulation planning. Stage 1 was completed in August 1972. Material presented in Chapter Four, including the typology of institutional and statewide articulation models, is representative of that portion of the total research project.

The major portion of *Middleman in Higher Education* is devoted to evaluating articulation models identified in Stage 1 of the Esso Education Foundation project. Such review and analysis was last reported nationally by Knoell-Medsker in 1964 at the conclusion of a project conducted by them at the Center for the Study of Higher Education, University of California, Berkeley. This comprehensive study was followed by a national project to improve transfer relationships between two- and four-year colleges supported by the Esso Education Foundation.

The 1966 *Report of the National Project for Improvement of Articulation Between Two-Year and Four-Year Colleges* identified problem areas and major activities associated with transfer, and offered guidelines to resolve transfer problems. Most of the issues presented in this report are alive today. Many of the questions continue to be debated, often heatedly, whenever and wherever school and college people gather. Among the important questions are the following:

> *Admissions.* Should public four-year colleges and universities maintain an open-door admission policy for transfer students; i.e., admit all transfer students who have earned at least a C average in junior college, irrespective of the likelihood of their succeeding?

Evaluation of Transfer Courses. What is the major purpose of evaluating junior college courses presented by transfer applicants? How much credit should junior college students be allowed to transfer? Should D grades transfer?

Curriculum Planning. What steps can be taken to avoid loss of time and credit by junior college students who transfer during a period of curriculum change?

Advising, Counseling, and Other Student Personnel Services. What should be done to improve academic advising of transfer students? What special orientation do transfer students need and how may it be effectively provided?

Articulation Programs. When the number of institutions precludes direct representation from each one, how can the desired representation be attained? Should articulation machinery be voluntary or legally mandated? Is there a need for both institutional and statewide articulation activities? How can good communication be achieved? [*Guidelines for Improving Articulation Between Junior and Senior Colleges,* 1966]

In addition to a review of current transfer relationships and an evaluation of current models, *Middleman in Higher Education* presents historical perspectives, relationships between high schools and community colleges, and a special chapter on directions and predictions for Canada.

This volume has grown from my many years of experience as teacher and administrator in community colleges and in corresponding roles at the University of California. I have written it to fill a gap in the literature on articulation, a subject of importance to educators at all levels. The book deals with the complex and crucial questions being asked with increasing intensity by high schools, community colleges, and universities.

Middleman in Higher Education exposes the plight of the transfer student and indicates possible solutions to the most critical problems he encounters. Major attention is given to a state-by-state account of recent developments in articulation and coordination, particularly efforts to systematize transfer policies. The analysis of articulation models should be valuable to educators responsible for improving articulation at the institutional level and to those in statewide leadership positions. Sections on changing practices in admission, orientation, student evaluation, and other areas should be of interest to instructors as well as to general administrators in universities and community colleges.

I anticipate that the "Summary of Articulation Policies in the Fifty States" will serve as a quick reference in meetings where comparative information on activities in other states is needed. In Chapter Four, articulation policies and procedures are shown by kind. Thus, the reader is allowed in these contrasting sections of the book to find his information from either of two directions. Until further studies are made, I hope this work will remain the standard reference on articulation.

A note on references: References for Chapters Four through Seven are situated at the end of each state discussion. References for Chapter Eight are at the end of the chapter. All other references may be found in the Bibliography at the end of the book.

Many individuals have provided significant suggestions during the preparation of *Middleman in Higher Education*. I am particularly grateful to Dorothy M. Knoell for her advice and counsel; to James L. Wattenbarger, a member of my committee for the articulation research project who, in addition to writing the Foreword, made valuable contributions to the manuscript; and to my colleague Dennis R. W. Wing, who assisted in the preparation of Chapter Eight. I am also indebted to educators throughout the country, over 160 in all, who provided material on articulation in the fifty states. The completion of this work was made possible by a grant from the Esso Education Foundation.

This book is dedicated to my wife, Ruth.

Los Angeles   Frederick C. Kintzer
January 1973

Contents

Foreword *by James L. Wattenbarger*   vii

Preface   xi

ONE: BACKGROUND   1

1. History   5

2. From High School to Community College   17

3. From Community College to University   26

TWO: THE ARTICULATION SCENE   33

4. Formal and Legal Policies   35

5. State System Policies   52

6. Voluntary Agreements Among Institutions   96

7. Developments in Other States   107

8. The Canadian Scene   127

9. Directions and Predictions   143

    Summary of Articulation Policies in the Fifty States   163

    Bibliography   173

    Index   180

Middleman in Higher Education

Improving Articulation among
High School, Community College,
and Senior Institutions

✿✿✿✿✿✿✿ PART I ✿✿✿✿✿✿✿

BACKGROUND

In performing its traditional transfer function, the community college acts as middleman in the educational system. More an open door than a selective institution, the community college generally accepts any high school graduates within its district. It attempts to prepare those showing academic ability for advanced study in senior colleges and universities. As working agreements among institutions are necessary if students are going to move smoothly through the educational system, articulation becomes the vital link to ensure qualified students an open door to the next level.

Articulation is one of the many confusing terms in the vocabulary of education. In this volume, the term *articulation* is specifically related to the method or process of joining together. It is a procedure that should provide a continuous, smooth flow of students from grade to grade and school to school. The need to develop a systematic procedure for student progress, with particular reference to integration of instructional programs, is implicit in the transfer process. In its broadest meaning, articulation refers to interrelationships among the various levels and segments of an educational system as well as among off-campus quasieducational institutions and activities. Segments of an educational system may be considered

1

well articulated if these interrelationships operate as a unified process.

Attitudes are important here—the willingness or reluctance of responsible personnel to enter voluntarily into cooperative planning agreements, placing the student ahead of administrative expediency. Success of the transfer process depends on continued, close interinstitutional communication and cooperation. Sacrifice of an institutional advantage is sometimes necessary to maintain a fair and flexible articulation system.

While centered on the student-services division of an institution, administration of an articulation program involves other offices, including instruction and institutional relations. Maximum cooperation is indeed necessary if this process is to assure a continuous flow of students and protect the integrity of both sending and receiving institutions. As an equalizer of post-high school educational opportunities, the community college offers help and encouragement to those who show academic promise but are not prepared for college work.

A weakness in basic skills, primarily reading, frequently leads to failure. A student from Foothill College, California, down 10 grade points after three terms at the University of California, attributed her lack of success to slow and inefficient reading. As a poor reader, she invariably froze on examinations and soon began to doubt her ability to succeed. She entered a special intensive summer class in reading improvement at Foothill. After one term of regular work, she was a B+ student at the community college and had regained considerable interest in continuing her college education.

The community college is involved in another type of remediation—salvaging a potential top performer who washed out of the senior institution in his first attempt and repairing the defeatist attitude that invariably accompanies failure. Transferring from a four-year college or university to a two-year college, the reverse transfer or drop-back pattern, is a recent and increasingly common phenomenon. State directors of community college education have indicated a growing concern for the increasing number of senior-to-junior college transfers. Data to substantiate this information is unfortunately sketchy. Only a few states keep records of reverse transfers.

The reverse-transfer trend was described in an analysis of 1967–1968 undergraduate students in Illinois and reported in a widely circulated booklet (Illinois Council on Articulation, 1971). The analysis showed that public junior colleges were receiving more transfer students than they were sending. Also, more students were transferring from private four-year institutions to public two-year colleges than to public four-year schools. The Illinois report further showed that transfer students do not necessarily leave the senior colleges and universities because of academic failure. About one-half had been dropped from public four-year colleges. The remaining 50 percent undoubtedly left, many returning to the community colleges, for reasons other than scholastic failure. While statewide figures are not available for succeeding years, Illinois leaders suggest that the reverse-transfer trend continues to be significant. A similar report was received from North Carolina, where in fall 1971 reverse transfers exceeded regular transfers. Although regular transfers outnumbered reverse transfers overall in 1971, the "drop down" group remained substantial in that state.

Dissatisfaction with university courses, content and sequence of classes, and teaching may well be leading reasons for returning home. Because the community college is generally dedicated to relevant curricula and instructional effectiveness, it has tremendous opportunities to serve this dissatisfied group.

Emotional immaturity rather than intellectual inability is often a major factor in the failure of lower-division university students. This situation is dramatically illustrated by the story of an electrical engineering major at Foothill College, California, who reported that he felt lost at the University of California. He made little attempt to develop consistent study habits. Contacts with other Foothill students who had experienced similar difficulties helped to revive his educational drive.

A girl who found success at Taft College, California, demonstrated that through personal attention a community college can help a student regain self-confidence. She ranked seventeenth in her high school class of 192, scored in the top percentile of both the Cooperative English Test and the School-College Ability Test, did poorly at the University of California as an art major, and felt overwhelmed. She was allowed to enter Taft College on personal recognition of the dean of students, returned to the university after one term at Taft, and subsequently graduated as an art major. She hopes to qualify for the School of Environmental Design, University of California, Berkeley, for a second baccalaureate degree.

While some might agree that admitting the second-chance students, particularly the "university castoff," could weaken the academic standing of the school, being just as tough as the senior institution is unwise. The community college then "forfeits its identity and its opportunity to experiment in the development of a program most appropriate to it" (Medsker, 1960).

Compared to his university counterpart, a community college student ordinarily finds himself less a cog in the academic machinery and more involved with counselors and teachers on a personal basis. A recent graduate of Hartnell College, Salinas, California, is typical of many who respond to this personal interest. He entered the University of California with a good record in a small high school, was shy and retiring, did poorly in physics and chemistry. After a year of little progress, he entered Hartnell College on dean's permission and changed his major to economics. He won an award as best economics student of the year and also lettered in basketball. The student graduated from Hartnell and ultimately from California Polytechnical College with a degree in business administration.

A small-college atmosphere is not necessarily related to size. Students interviewed at Los Angeles City College (one of the largest community colleges) commented that the counseling center is aways open, instructors are available twenty-four hours a day, and almost everybody crosses the quad between classes.

In this area of personal and individual opportunity the senior institution can learn most from the community college. Here the two-year college makes its greatest contribution. All institutions —most of all the universities—need to develop and practice the art of caring. The transfer student is particularly vulnerable to the lack of caring. Invariably he arrives with inadequate information and receives, by and large, little orientation when he gets to the senior institution.

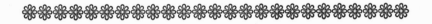

History

Articulation until very recently has largely been a one-way situation, a series of policies and procedures dictated by senior institutions. Before 1960, coordinated efforts to improve the plight of the transfer student were almost nonexistent. While articulation agreements between senior colleges and universities and high schools were generally well developed, programs centering attention on the two-year college graduate were scarce. Only in states where the junior college movement had taken root (in California, Illinois, Texas, and Washington) were graduates sufficiently numerous to necessitate some coordinated planning. In all states except California, transfer student applications could be processed individually.

Efforts of a few concerned educational leaders first bore fruit in 1957 in the creation of a national committee established by the Association of American Colleges and the American Association of Junior Colleges. A year later the American Association of Collegiate Registrars and Admissions Officers (under the inspirational guidance of Clyde Vroman) joined the original committee to form the Joint Committee on Junior and Senior Colleges.

Under the chairmanship of James L. Wattenbarger, the

Joint Committee developed guidelines for junior colleges and senior colleges and universities to facilitate transfer and in 1960 requested the Center for the Study of Higher Education at the University of California, Berkeley, to conduct studies on the characteristics and transfer problems of junior college graduates. This research effort, which resulted in two technical reports by Dorothy M. Knoell and Leland L. Medsker, published by the center in 1963–1964, was supported by the U.S. Office of Education. Their book *From Junior to Senior College,* published by the American Council on Education, was a reader's version of the technical reports and was released in 1966.

A fall 1960 transfer population in excess of 7300 students from ten states was the basic sample studied by Knoell and Medsker. The states and their senior institutions were selected according to specific criteria, including different types of organization and control, formal admission policies, and approximately a hundred or more transfers. Five types of senior institutions (forty-three in all) were chosen in each of the ten states: the major state universities (or the public university in each state with the longest record of university status); public institutions with primary emphasis on the preparation of teachers; other state colleges and universities with multiple functions; private universities; technical institutions. No attempt was made to involve certain junior colleges; 345, however, were represented in the comprehensive study. Ninety-one percent of the transfers came from junior colleges in ten selected states: California, Florida, Georgia, Illinois, Kansas, Michigan, New York, Pennsylvania, Texas, and Washington. The other 9 percent came from junior colleges scattered over thirty-three other states and the Canal Zone.

For the performance comparison portion of the study, the researchers dealt with a transfer group of slightly over 4000 without regard to the time of entrance in senior institutions granting the degrees (about 1200 had transferred before 1960) and approximately 3350 native students (those who had taken all their collegiate work in the senior institutions) who graduated with baccalaureate degrees in 1962.

The work of the Joint Committee climaxed in a series of state and regional conferences that led to the publication of the

Guidelines for Improving Articulation Between Junior and Senior College in 1966. These efforts were known as the National Project for Improvement of Articulation Between Two-Year and Four-Year Colleges and were directed by James H. Nelson. Financial support for the conferences was provided by the Esso Education Foundation. The Foundation also supported the preparation of *A Digest of Research Findings* prepared by Knoell for use in the National Project (Wattenbarger, 1966; Knoell and Medsker, 1965).

Although hastened by the explosive growth of community colleges in all sections of the country and by their general acceptance as partners in higher education, an acceleration of transfer activities in the late 1960s followed as a direct result of the Joint Committee efforts and the comprehensive research of Knoell and Medsker. The *Guidelines* developed by the Joint Committee is a basic reference in Kansas, Maryland, North Dakota, Ohio, Oklahoma, and Washington, where statewide articulation policies are being developed.

The final chapter in *From Junior to Senior College,* which provides the conclusions and implications of the authors' investigations, continues to be widely used. The authors called for the expansion of two-year colleges to approach the goal of equal opportunity. The open-door college, they commented, should continue to be the melting pot of higher education where every student has an opportunity to strive for the highest educational goal he believes he is capable of achieving. They further urged the development of master plans at the state level that would define institutional roles and plan coordinated curricula including transfer of occupational as well as academic programs. Knoell and Medsker suggested that proper matching of transfer student and institution is probably more important than matching freshman student and institution. The authors pointed out the general inadequacy of orientation programs for transfer students (a negative factor often reported in the *National Pilot Study,* made eight years later) and of counseling services at both the two- and four-year institution.

The Knoell-Medsker studies also gave considerable attention to the grading systems, pointing out that the use of grade point differentials as standards for evaluating the success of transfer students would become even less appropriate as community colleges serve an increasingly diverse population and universities inevitably become more selective.

In an eleven-point outline, Wattenbarger (1972) succinctly summarizes other interrelated contributions of the Knoell-Medsker research.

(1) In their academic work, students usually perform in a manner similar to their past patterns of accomplishment. Individuals however improve. It would therefore be prudent to avoid applying such generalizations to individual students in making decisions that determine their futures.

(2) Policies regarding probation and dismissal sometimes reflect poor decision-making procedures in the university and discrimination against transfer students. In many instances these are record-keeping rather than educational policies.

(3) Problems such as financial support, inadequate goals, and lack of self-confidence, which may have influenced students to select a two-year college near home to begin their college work, do not change when they become transfer students.

(4) Students who complete a two-year associate degree program in a community college may be expected to be more successful after transfer than those who move before completing the two years.

(5) Despite the availability of much information on the numbers, the characteristics, and the problems of students who transfer, most senior institutions have done little to examine their policies to determine how they discriminate against the transfer student.

(6) Academic bookkeeping procedures—for example, computing grade point averages into a single mean—have little validity in predicting desirable outcomes for a college education.

(7) If the success of a system of higher education in a state may be measured by low attrition rates and high graduation rates, then those states with effective articulation programs may be called most successful.

(8) Since restrictions on admission to the freshman class in many senior colleges and universities are often more rigorous than those for admission to the junior class, the community college serves as a second-chance institution for many highly motivated young

people. Those who successfully complete their first two years can continue toward their baccalaureate degrees usually without reference to their high school work.

(9) The complexity of articulation of programs will increase as additional specializations are developed.

(10) There is urgent need for constant contact among counselors in high schools, two-year colleges, and institutions granting baccalaureate degrees.

(11) The college population is highly mobile. Many students transfer from one four-year institution to another, from university to junior college and back again, and from junior to senior college.

These findings should be carefully considered when developing transfer agreements. The conclusions might in fact form the bases for guideline statements.

Pertinent to the major thrust of this volume, Knoell and Medsker concluded that present articulation machinery in many states and in many institutions is inadequate to solve the problems that will be brought on by an increasing volume of transfer students. Findings of a 1969 survey of admissions patterns by Willingham and Findikyan generally supported the final Knoell-Medsker conclusion. From questionnaire data returned by a representative group of 146 senior institutions and from transcripts of a sample of transfer students to each senior college or university, the authors reported both favorable and unfavorable situations in transfer admissions. While the junior college model was generally successful, the authors found some aspects of the transfer picture disturbing. Like the previously discussed researchers, Willingham and Findikyan warned that "there may often be considerable institutional inertia with respect to transfer admissions—inertia which must be overcome in order to make the accommodations necessary if a college wishes a substantial increase in transfer enrollment."

A comprehensive statement of transfer guidelines was produced under the general coordination of the National Project for Improvement of Articulation Between Two-Year and Four-Year Colleges. As indicated earlier in the chapter, the transfer guidelines were drafted at the conclusion of the Knoell-Medsker research and were refined and revised in a series of follow-up conferences in the ten states that had participated in the Knoell-Medsker studies. The principles presented in the guidelines were purposely stated in such general terms that the participating states could use them as bases for developing specific articulation policies and procedures. While these principles have not been widely used in developing state master plans, they have to a certain extent influenced statewide inter-segmental agreements, including the articulation agreements (detailed in Part Two) in California, Florida, Illinois, New York, and Oklahoma.

Willingham (1972) attempted to determine (through a series of informal telephone conversations with representatives of the forty-three institutions that participated in the Knoell-Medsker studies) if the guidelines for articulation were being followed. Little evidence of widespread application was reported. While results of the survey did not suggest a great amount of change, changes mentioned typically indicated a continuing move to more flexible policies.

Two additional studies on articulation should be mentioned: the *Nationwide Pilot Study on Articulation* (Kintzer, 1970) and a survey of transfer admissions, course credit, and transfer problems circulated to community college admissions officers by the American Association of Collegiate Registrars and Admissions Officers Junior-Senior College Relations Committee.

The first document, composed of a state-by-state profile, gave impetus to the three-stage project mentioned in the Preface of this volume. Material was obtained from eighty educators. State officials, college and university directors of admissions, registrars, and community college presidents and deans provided the commentary in five areas: background (historical development, current types and numbers of transfers, administrative patterns, and groups—devoted to articulation), philosophy, policies and procedures, problems, predictions.

The second study presented the results of a survey of community colleges, determining the current status of two-year college degrees and certificates as currency for transferring to senior institutions. The report was initially presented by Paul L. Scherer, admissions officer, University of California, Santa Barbara, at the spring 1972 meeting of the American Association of Collegiate Registrars and Admissions Officers (AACRAO) and was published in the 1972 summer edition of *College and University*. The survey was made under the general direction of Jack L. Hoover, director of admissions, University of Montana (chairman of the AACRAO committee). Most of the 461 public and 129 private colleges returning the comprehensive inquiry form were in states where changes in requirements and procedures were being proposed or established by some one of the controlling agencies of higher education.

The major finding was the poor communication common in many states—procedures reported as common practices by some colleges were apparently unknown to neighboring institutions. This lack of understanding existed among both senior institutions and community colleges, state agencies in higher education systems, and self-organized groups such as community college associations and specialist groups representing all institutions in higher education. Florida was the only state where all community college respondents knew that a statewide articulation agreement existed. Surprisingly, only half the thirty community colleges reporting from Illinois were aware of the agreement (described in Chapter Four of this book).

Except for the several landmark studies just described, material on articulation is conspicuously scarce. As one would expect, the several books recognized as authoritative works on the two-year college published between 1950 and 1965 offered only brief discussions of articulation. In fact, the word *articulation* was seldom used. The Medsker volume (1960), which makes extensive reference to transfer problems, to transfer student performance and retention, and to faculty attitudes toward the transfer phenomenon, is the only one of the early books on the two-year college to make more than cursory reference to articulation.

Books published since 1965 however make specific references to transfer admissions: Thornton (1966) outlines problems of articulation; Gleazer (1968) includes several references to transfer to four-year colleges; Johnson (1969) examines junior college responsibility for preparing students for upper division; Cohen and associates (1971) provide a section on articulation studies; and Medsker and Tillery (1971) are among the first to give some attention to articulation downward from the community college.

Curriculum articulation between two- and four-year institutions has changed considerably in terms of principles on which acceptance policies are based. Shifts in the history of course transferability in California illustrate this changing scene. The junior college movement initiated in California by the Caminetti Act of 1907 permitted the establishment of junior colleges (in high school districts) with curriculum limited to courses parallel to those given in lower-division programs of the University of California. Excerpts from the *Junior College Circular* issued in 1915 with an extended statement by Dean Alexis F. Lange, Department of Education of the University of California, presented the university policies on transfer admissions; exact course parallelism was required. Credit for the work of a year was given on the basis of credentials from other colleges, including junior colleges. If evidence showed that an affiliated junior college was providing a full year of work beyond the high school, the University of California authorized thirty-two units (a few more in engineering) and tried to distribute these credits to satisfy requirements for what was called the Junior Certificate portion of the bachelor's degree (Spindt, 1954).

Acceptance of credits and courses remained provisional without guarantee; they were transferable only on individual review until a formal affiliation policy was started in 1923. The University Board of Admissions invited junior colleges to become affiliates of the university—to be lower-division extensions. If affiliated, the junior college was assured credit for lower-division courses offered. Several specific features of the policy of affiliation clearly identified the extension status of the fledging junior colleges and the exact course parallelism required. Students admitted to a transfer program in an affiliate college had to be eligible for admission to the university. Teachers selected by the junior college had to be approved by the president of the university, and a course had to be inspected and approved by the appropriate university department before credits were guaranteed. Teacher load was also subject to approval by university officials. Another interesting detail of this agreement was that applicants from affiliated junior colleges were eligible for admission even though their grades might be well below a c average. This clause was obviously not a risk to the University since affiliated junior colleges were in effect University campuses.

The affiliation arrangement lasted only three years and involved a maximum of eight junior colleges. Soon after the arrangement was dissolved by mutual consent, the practice of accepting only exactly parallel courses began to loosen. The shift in requirement to similar or equivalent courses was signaled in an address given in 1930 by President Robert Gordon Sproul to the annual meeting of the National Association of Junior Colleges: "The challenge of the next decade is an opportunity for all of us, an opportunity for the junior college to place a premium upon initiative and variation rather than upon conformity, a challenge to the university to make an examination of the first two years of its course in order that the most may be made of them. It will not be sufficient for either of us to follow the old lines, even if they are better than some of us think they are."

By 1955, the principle of strict course parallelism had given way in most sections of the country to equivalency as the base for course acceptability. Again the University of California illustrates the changing emphasis. The criteria statement released by E. W. Strong, dean of the Berkeley campus College of Letters and Science (1951), particularly the section on acceptability of variant courses (those not parallel to university courses), and the companion document, released by J. W. Robson, dean of the Los Angeles campus College of Letters and Science (1952), are based on an equivalency or similarity relationship.

Now developments in package acceptance, including some vocational work that will be detailed in Part Two, indicate that the attitude of surveillance and control on the part of senior institutions might well be giving way to one of peer relationship in curriculum articulation. This general change is developing most rapidly where the success of transfer students has resulted in a general acceptance of community college transfer programs—where community colleges are initiating or are soon likely to initiate and formally name transfer courses and patterns. Such a procedure is currently followed in California, where community colleges identify transfer courses that are annually checked and invariably endorsed by the university-wide director of admissions and registrar. In effect the university is saying: "We will accept as transfer what you say is transfer." Full in-faith acceptance of the associate degree, including technical-vocational credits and without regard for the high school record, is the ultimate position yet to be achieved.

During this period of rapidly increasing recognition of institutional integrity, community colleges should not be required to imitate the senior institutions in transfer course content and sequences. On the contrary, they should be encouraged to develop their own programs with an educational value at least equal to those in the lower divisions of universities to which most students expect to transfer. If a university program stresses quantitative thinking, logical reasoning, and other specific intellectual skills, then the community college should insist that transfers achieve a similar kind and level of accomplishment. If a university program demands a wide breadth of experience and depth of understanding in a particular major field, the community college transfer program must be equally exacting. Work in the two institutions need not and should not be parallel or imitative, but equal rigor is certainly advisable if the transfer student is to have a fair opportunity to compete in the upper division. Few community colleges however have faced the obligation of providing equal opportunity to succeed.

Few states have recognized the two-year college as a bona fide lower-division institution, and few have supported a plan to provide equal access to upper-division and graduate education for the transfer student. Several states (California, Florida, Georgia, Illinois, New York, and Oklahoma) have complied partially or shown on paper commitments to one or both obligations.

As for transfer student performance, considerable evidence is available to support the generalization that students of equal ability perform equally well regardless of the college route taken. Conclusions emerging from studies dating from 1928 (Mitchell and Eells at Stanford University) to 1954 (Martorana and Williams at the State College of Washington—now Washington State University) indicated that the record of junior college transfers was approximately the same as that of transfers from four-year colleges and of native students. Transfers excelled occasionally. They usually showed a 0.50 drop (approximately) in their grade averages in the first term after transfer but recovered that loss by the time of graduation. Transfer students, in these early studies, retained the relative standing that they held before transfer. Those who originally had high records tended to remain top students; those who were relatively low tended to remain so at the senior institutions. Wide variation was noted in the findings at different universities as well as between junior colleges and the same university. This situation was due in part to the lack of articulation agreements. (Efforts to develop transfer policies cooperatively were still in the embryonic stage.) But evidence was clear in these early studies that junior colleges were salvaging many students for successful careers in universities.

Approximately a decade later results of Knoell and Medsker's comprehensive report (1964) of about 7300 former two-year college students who attended senior colleges and universities in ten states showed that grade point average differences between transfer and native students were only slight at graduation. Commenting on persistence, the authors indicated that transfers were just as efficient as natives in the total number of semesters attended and units earned in satisfaction of baccalaureate-degree requirements. They concluded that junior colleges were providing an important avenue to the attainment of the baccalaureate degree for many students who would not otherwise have been able to undertake such programs.

In a comprehensive review of approximately twenty transfer studies with thirty-three sets of data, beginning in 1922, Hills found considerable agreement that the transfer student usually experiences a transfer shock—a fractional grade point drop in the first term in upper division, which he recovers in succeeding terms—and that the transfer student remains somewhat below his native counterpart (Hills, 1965). Specifically, twenty-two of the thirty-three sets of data showed that native students did better than the transfers and seven indicated no difference in performance.

According to studies conducted by Nickens, the transfer shock and recovery phenomenon popularized by Hills is caused by factors other than transfer itself. Nickens suggests that transfer shock is related to grading practices and other factors and that recovery is as much associated with natives as transfers (Nickens, 1972).

Findings similar to those of the Knoell-Medsker study and those summarized by Bird (1956) were reported in a transfer-native study conducted at the University of California, Los Angeles. Approximately 1800 freshmen entering in 1960 were compared with 800 students transferring in 1962 from California public junior colleges. Entering with a 2.85 grade point average, after one university semester transfers dropped to 2.35. After three semesters however the group had improved to a 2.63 average. Grade point differences between the two groups progressively diminished with each succeeding semester—0.34, 0.26, and 0.15. While the study was not carried to graduation, groups at that point would likely have been separated by less than a tenth of a grade. Students ineligible because of inadequate high school grades were represented in the transfer group, giving added support to the quality of California public junior colleges in terms of the success of their students at UCLA (Kintzer, 1967).

Much research has been conducted on a wide variety of characteristics of two-year college students. Cross (1968) synthesized the findings of major studies since 1960. Of these efforts, research conducted by Medsker and Trent in 1964–1965, the Project TALENT studies completed by Cooley and Becker in 1966, and the SCOPE research (*School to College: Opportunities for Postsecondary Education*) directed by Tillery and reported by him and others in 1966 and 1968 are the most diversified and comprehensive. Yet comparatively little attention has been given to transfer-native student success comparisons since the 1964 Knoell-Medsker studies. Research reported in this specific area is invariably restricted to single disciplines and confined to single institutions. Available evidence however supports the contention that community college lower divisions have in general proved their worth; the quality of such preparation should be widely recognized.

Research on all aspects of the transfer student and the transfer phenomenon is an obvious and immediate need if articulation agreements forthcoming in state after state are to be successful. At the same time, priority must also be given to institutional relationships through personal contacts between and among all staff levels if agreements are to be mutually acceptable.

 2

From High School
to
Community College

From the community college perspective, articulation is often viewed as an upward movement to senior colleges or universities. The importance of downward communication with high schools is slighted or completely overlooked and remains generally unreported. Community colleges are prone to concentrate on sending students to senior colleges and to neglect their responsibilities as receiving institutions. Effective articulation between two-year colleges and high schools is necessary if the needs of communities are to be served. Reorganization in community college governance and administration offer both challenges and opportunities in initiating and maintaining smooth articulation downward.

Common administrative ties characteristic of the K-14 organization, in which a high school and a junior college were in a

17

single district, have virtually disappeared. Each institution is likely to pursue its independent role. Establishment of separate districts creates a face-to-face relationship between high school and community college—a favorable climate for developing articulation. Secondary schools and two-year colleges share equal responsibility for creating a team relationship.

Despite the formal separation, the advantages of continued education still remain. Wattenbarger (1972) translates these advantages into opportunities. He states that there are numerous opportunities for subject-matter scope and sequence planning with local high school faculties, unlimited opportunities to provide for gifted students to accelerate their educational progress while maintaining important contacts with their peer groups in social development. The community college may share with the high schools in providing numerous community services to the entire district. In all these activities, according to Wattenbarger, the community college must assume a role of active leadership.

Difficulties of downward articulation are increased in states where two-year colleges have an open-door policy. This permits increasing numbers of high school dropouts and university dropdowns to seek second opportunities. Special programs for the disadvantaged and handicapped are other complicating factors, as these two groups are particularly vulnerable to breakdowns in articulation. The open door more easily becomes a revolving door for the disadvantaged.

Other developments militate against smooth high school–community college articulation: early high school completion—the community college must fill in the awkward time gap; the rapidly increasing practice of awarding credit by examination in high school; expansion of career education in high schools; and lowering the legal age to eighteen.

Adult education presents additional communication difficulties. Programs for adults in many states may be maintained by high school districts, by community college districts, or by both, thereby increasing competition and diminishing communication.

Communication between community colleges and high schools becomes especially difficult in overlapping programs where high school enrollees are also part-time community college students.

Passage of the Veysey Bill in California has enabled up to 15 percent of the eleventh- and twelfth-grade students to attend community college classes. Their reported success (Plusch, 1967) has been due to cooperative efforts, particularly between high school and college counseling divisions.

Counseling offices must be linked in a successful articulation relationship, and several techniques for coordinating programs have recently been reported. Part-time high school counselors are hired at Miami-Dade Junior College in Florida to identify and register high school students and adults who might benefit from college classes. Some high school counselors receive intensive training and serve evenings and weekends in certain Dade County high schools. Junior college students train as counseling aides and assist regular counselors at the high schools from which they were graduated. The program continues to be successful in student services and has provided a communication link between high school and junior college counseling staffs (Smith, 1970).

Responsibility for improving the articulation process also rests with the high school. Publication and distribution of a college handbook, frequently used to encourage student planning, is one of the best methods for maintaining communication with surrounding community colleges. "Thinking About College: Some Basic Considerations for Student and Parent," a publication developed by the Mt. Diablo Unified School District, California, includes an introduction to area community colleges and their offerings. One of the most complete handbooks for students, parents, and counselors, *Mapping Your Education,* is issued by the Oregon-Washington Commission through Abbott, Kerns and Bell Company of Portland. Such handbooks are rich sources of current information for school counselors who play a key role in influencing student vocational choices.

While only fragmentary information is available on programs and activities to improve articulation downward from the community college, scattered reports have been received from several states.

California. A program is maintained at City College of San Francisco. Operating under a specially funded summer project since 1967, high school students and high school teacher–counselors are brought to the city college. Students are enrolled in regular college courses and helped in selecting realistic occupational objectives. Teacher-counselors participate in special workshops designed to improve techniques of vocational guidance and to orient them to city college semiprofessional and trade programs (San Francisco Unified School District, 1968).

An important method of building downward articulation is practiced at Pasadena City College, California. Certified high school counselors are hired for evening employment at the college counseling offices when registration activity is heaviest. They quickly learn college admissions and counseling policies and procedures and become authoritative sources of information at their local high schools (Lewis, 1970). Six other approaches to improving downward articulation used at Pasadena City College are briefly outlined by Lewis:

First, advanced academic or vocational students from the high schools, juniors and seniors, may enroll concurrently at the college for one or two classes. This has been an excellent means of articulating course content and also of improving communication between the high schools and the college.

Second, a quarterly newsletter giving admissions and instruction information circulates to all the district high schools. Some of the high schools ask for sufficient copies to place the newsletter in each homeroom or guidance room. This has proved an exemplary means of communication.

Third, subject area conferences are productive articulation devices for the junior high school, senior high school, and junior college. At Pasadena City College, departments have sponsored conferences in their subject areas, inviting teachers from neighboring junior and senior high schools to confer with the college faculty.

Fourth, the high school advisory committee, which consists of the assistant principal for guidance or the guidance coordinator from each of nine public and four private high schools in the Pasadena Area Junior College District, considers all matters related to improved admissions and counseling procedures. It meets twice a year with the college administrative dean for student personnel services.

Fifth, each Pasadena City College counselor is responsible

for regular invited visits to high schools to improve the flow of information. Counselors, department chairmen, and faculty provide a total PCC Night at a high school, presenting the curriculum available at the College.

Sixth, the president of the college regularly schedules meetings of the six unified school-district superintendents. Matters of common interest are discussed, including instructional programs, use of the college planetarium or computer science facilities, the calendar, and related matters.

Specific opportunities for communication between high school and community college representatives are provided by the California Articulation Conference. This organization (described more fully in Chapter Six) meets each May to review relationships between higher education and secondary schools. High school and community college delegates meet twice during the two-day conference to hear progress reports and to work out solutions to problems. While subject-matter and service-area liaison committees contribute most, communication at the intersegmental meetings is direct and pertinent.

Colorado. Articulation activity between community colleges and high schools is coordinated by the Colorado Council on High School–College Relations. The council consists of members from secondary schools, community colleges, senior colleges, and universities, and it publishes an annual handbook. Otero Junior College (in La Junta) contracts with the city schools to provide vocational education for the area.

Florida. Most community colleges work closely with the high schools in their own district. Seniors are encouraged to visit community college campuses and arrangements are made in several community colleges for seniors to begin their college work while still in high school. Counselors are employed for summer work in the community college; occupational information is made available to students in the middle schools and in junior high and senior high schools (Wattenbarger, 1972).

Missouri. At Forest Park Community College in the St. Louis Junior College District, junior high school students visit the campus on Saturdays for a general view of the college and are given book covers and other mementos.

New York. Full opportunity programs operated by community colleges guarantee to every recent high school graduate and to every veteran separated from the armed services during the preceding year admission to a full-time program geared to the individual's interest and achievement level. The program requires that individual colleges submit plans that show articulation efforts with high schools. Some colleges have developed agreements with cooperating high schools allowing students to attend both college and high school and to receive college credit before completing high school.

Under a unique program of urban centers and cooperative community college centers developed in New York, students completing urban center–college adapter programs move directly into regular associate-degree programs at the supervising community college. Some colleges have developed plans with cooperating high schools enabling students to attend both college and high school and to receive college credit for work completed at the college prior to high school graduation.

The City University of New York (under a program of the State University of New York) publishes a *Community College Handbook* providing information about its six community colleges. The handbook is given wide circulation in secondary school systems. An insert on transfer policies for career students is particularly valuable.

Virginia. The Virginia community college system issues *Counseling Information,* a publication intended as guidance for high school counselors. The booklet includes facts about the twenty-six community colleges (including campuses of multiunit districts). The outline of admission steps in community colleges is particularly effective.

Articulation with the secondary schools is one of the current priorities of New River Community College in Dublin, Virginia. The college offers opportunities for secondary school students to enroll in classes, particularly summer classes. Only positive credit is recorded; no permanent record is kept of unsatisfactory performance. Credit is applicable toward degrees at the college.

Counselors, the admissions director, and financial aids coordinator spend 30 to 40 percent of their time visiting local high schools.

They supervise administration of the Comparative Guidance and Placement Test both in the secondary schools and on the college campus. In turn, the public schools are encouraged to arrange college tours. Each tour has a specific goal—career orientation and supplementary lectures in art, science, ecology, or other subjects.

New River Community College makes a positive attempt to coordinate technical programs with the public schools in and around Dublin, and has sponsored a number of formal articulation conferences. An account of these efforts to smooth the transition from secondary vocational programs to occupational-technical programs at the community college is found in a May 1972 report.

Washington. Community colleges submit reports at regular intervals to the state board for community colleges on high school relations activities. The reports describe a variety of activities and programs for establishing communication and improving relations with high schools. Several of the more innovative ideas reflect a statewide recognition that a successful program of high school articulation is the lifeblood of the community college. Yakima Valley College has an agreement with local schools for off-campus employment of college students. Shoreline Community College conducts oceanography and marine biology institutes for elementary and junior high school teachers. A team of Wenatchee Valley College representatives travels to high schools to meet with incoming students and their parents. Bellevue Community College offers learning-center facilities to high school students with learning problems. The "three-six program" at Spokane Community College provides opportunities for high school students to take occupational classes between 3 P.M. and 6 P.M.

Universities maintaining offices school services or relations help in various ways to improve high school–community college articulation. The bulletins they issue serve as clearinghouses for high school–community college conferences, often sponsored and held on the university campus. These publications carry relevant articles on articulation; a list of these will be found in Chapter Nine.

Regional accrediting agencies in varying degrees help to improve articulation. Since recognition through full membership in a regional agency is invariably a cherished institutional goal, the agency holds the whip hand. The self-studies required periodically are strong incentives promoting comprehensive self-evaluations and total institutional involvement. Those institutions following to the letter the recommendations of their regional accrediting agency will improve communication between schools and advance the effectiveness of the articulation process.

In its "Self-Study Outline for Two-Year Institutions," the New England Association of Colleges and Secondary Schools, Inc., requires answers to three questions: In what ways, if any, does your institution cooperate with other institutions or groups of institutions in educational offerings? In other areas? Are arrangements of this type contemplated in the future? Both the southern and middle states associations maintain standing committees on school–college relations.

Secondary school administrators are required by the accrediting commission for secondary schools of the western association to attach statements to accreditation applications describing what provisions are made for continuity of student progress through articulation with feeder schools and with schools receiving their graduates. The community college commission bases questions on the following assumptions, considered elements of community college–high school articulation: High school students and even elementary pupils are familiar with the educational opportunities and community services of the community college. The faculty of the high school and community college are in close communication, and are working together on curriculum and instruction to meet the needs of students. Student personnel staffs of the community college and the high schools work closely to simplify transfers. The community college and the high schools work cooperatively to assist disadvantaged or minority students and to provide programs for the educationally alienated of all ages. The community college has information about the economic, educational, and social characteristics of the area to understand the nature of the people it serves.

Career education offers special opportunities for strengthening community college–high school relations. The term *career education,* as presented in Title X of the Education Amendments Act of 1972, should strengthen the communication link between high schools and community colleges. As described by Muirhead, career education "recognized the career implications of all education and the educational nature of all experience." Career education, by definition, further "minimizes credentialism or the idea that the only noble path to success and happiness is an education leading to a traditional four-year degree or beyond" (Muirhead, 1973).

The landmark legislation also stresses the role of the high school in career preparation by the use of terms "all education" and "all experiences" and by direct references to "career ladder opportunities." Obviously the act has a heavy impact on the relationships among the federal government, school systems, and the higher education community.

Action programs are being initiated to improve career program articulation between high schools and community colleges. In Los Angeles, for example, where career courses are offered by the seventy-three high shools in the Los Angeles School District and the eight community colleges in the Los Angeles Community College District, a model program is being developed. The primary goal is to articulate college, secondary, and community resources concerned with occupational education and thus to continue career programs on a sequential learning basis. Success of the plan will depend largely on how well communication is maintained among the representatives of high schools, community colleges, four-year colleges, government agencies, and community resource groups (Simonds, 1971).

Articulation in education is definitely a team process—a series of complex and interlocking formal relationships between schools. As described throughout this book, articulation is also an attitude. Differences in institutional philosophy are not always identifiable, while individual prejudices are often hard to overcome and invariably indicate a lack of communication. Willingness to compromise extreme positions and to tolerate the views of others is essential if transfer relationships between high schools and community colleges are to succeed. The community college should expect no better treatment from universities than it is willing to extend to high schools.

3

From Community
College to University

Community college people vigorously advocate that the privilege of faculties to establish curriculum should apply equally to them—that since their institutions are heavily engaged in lower-divison education, they should be able to name transfer courses and to build their transfer programs to meet requirements set by law or by senior institutions. They contend that they deserve guarantees that credits will not later be jeopardized by arbitrary and capricious whims of university faculties.

In general, however, community colleges are simply not free to develop their own programs. Pressure to conform to university course outlines hinders the community college in designing work appropriate to students needs and in experimenting with new curricula and teaching techniques. In many states, community college courses must parallel the lower-division patterns of the senior colleges. This requirement can become unreasonably complex, and the student, after all, is likely to remain caught in the middle.

Community college people claim (and it does happen) that universities sometimes ignore or fail to recognize that transfer students make comparably good grades at the university. They continue to require higher grades of the next group of transfers for admission. This treatment, the community colleges claim, is unjustified and is an expression of prejudice on the part of university admission personnel. They ask simply that facts of transfer student success be recognized. They also point out that universities should provide orientation for transfers as they do much more uniformly for freshmen.

In addition, community college people accuse the universities and senior colleges of impeding smooth articulation by formalizing curricular changes arbitrarily and suddenly, rather than cooperatively and with reasonable lead time (perhaps eighteen months); insisting on detailed community college course investigation and an exact equivalence of courses; refusing to accept occupational courses, which, in fact, may have value for baccalaureate degrees (data-processing, agriculture, police science, aviation, real estate), and putting limitations on the amount of credit granted in certain fields (business education, physical education, music); refusing to accept a transfer course because of an openly expressed feeling that it is inferior to the university counterpart; shifting their own courses from lower to upper division and in general obliterating the separation between these two divisions while holding community colleges to specific definitions of lower and upper division; allowing colleges, schools, or departments within the university to set widely differing requirements for major fields and for graduation; examining community college courses but not those of senior colleges whose students seek transfer, thereby operating on a double standard; requiring a higher grade point average for transfer students than for native students to enter upper-division work; not providing orientation programs for the transfer student; making the associate degree, where it is accepted at all, an absolute requirement for university admission; limiting enrollment of transfer students in certain programs. For all these reasons, community college people are understandably pressing for liberalized transfer arrangements.

For their part, senior college representatives invariably maintain that evaluation of junior college courses is the prerogative of baccalaureate-granting institutions, whose professors, by long-standing tradition, establish curriculum and set standards for that degree. This obligation, university professors strongly feel, assures consistent academic quality by disallowing credit for courses that do not match university standards. They are quick to point out that if transfer students are to have equal opportunities to succeed in upper-division work, the academic solids taken in community colleges must be of uniform quality before blanket approval can be accorded to them. Such apprehension appears most frequently in preparation for upper-division work in the major field.

University professors claim that two-year colleges because of inexperience mix subcollege with college material in courses that are classified for transfer, and the professors feel they have no control over this dilution of content. They also believe that community colleges develop transfer courses without consultation with senior institutions; fail to establish a system for managing articulation within the institution itself; rely on informal communication between community college professors and university professors rather than between counselors or other designated articulation specialists; fail to offer prerequisites for a course normally regarded as intermediate or specialized or, if prerequisites are determined, fail to mention them in requests for recognition of the course; fail to clarify course content; fail to notify students that subcollege and vocational courses do not transfer; fail to provide adequate transfer guidelines to students either through the counseling staff or in print.

All segments of public higher education share responsibility for difficulties that tend to weaken articulation of courses and credits. Many problems (credit and course acceptability in particular) pertain specifically to "bookkeeping"—grading systems, details of registration and admissions, credit evaluation. But bookkeeping problems may, in Wattenbarger's (1972) words, "be symptoms of much more deep-seated philosophical positions . . . centered around questions of institutional integrity, faculty competencies, restricted admissions policies, equivalency of courses, planning of programs, individual counseling procedures, student activities, and occupational objectives." Differences in philosophy are clearly identifiable. Universities, partly because of their increasingly selective roles, maintain exacting entrance requirements and generally insist on rigorous academic performance. Community colleges generally accept students where they find them and permit them to progress under more flexible standards and less arduous competition and often at a slower pace. Other difficulties are due to public and state expectations for two-year and four-year institutions. Some differences on articulation suggest the need for more and better trained personnel. But all indicate a lack of communication. Because communication is vital, few articulation problems are permanently solved. As Wattenbarger (1972) suggests, "As soon as a workable procedure is reached and/or a decision made clear and certain of understanding on the part of all concerned, there are personnel changes; new individuals who have no common background in reaching solutions begin to make decisions and thereby to affect the entire process."

Accreditation can also be a roadblock to efficient articulation. In fact, one experienced official calls accreditation "the most vexing factor in the transfer admission process" (Wilson, 1970). Senior institutions are often more concerned with the accreditation of the two-year college that supplies transfer students than with the status of the high school that sends freshmen. Transfer applicants from unaccredited colleges are invariably allowed no transfer credit. As Wilson (1970) wisely observes, "We should be more concerned about our *admission* of students (particularly from new, yet-to-be accredited institutions) than about our *acceptance of their credits* once we have admitted them."

Difficulties also occur in working with professional-school accrediting agencies, which often do not allow credits from lower-division institutions to apply toward professional degrees. A few universities have been working to include credit for community college courses, especially in business and journalism, within the professional-school accreditation agreements.

Two-year open-door colleges located in the economically deprived sections of the inner city face peculiar articulation problems because of their responsibility for encouraging disadvantaged students. These schools need the understanding and cooperation of nearby universities that share similar problems—including having relatively large numbers of marginal or low-aptitude applicants and high failure rates among those matriculated.

Although all these problems must be dealt with through co-operative action, the vital issue is seldom discussed. This broad question, largely unresolved, was raised originally by Bird (1956): "What shall be meant, then, by 'the kind and quality of education' that advances the transfer student properly toward the four-year college goals? Shall it mean strict course-by-course parallels? . . . Not necessarily. . . . The thing that does seem necessary is that the junior college programs of study for transfer students shall be equivalent in educational value . . . in terms of the senior college purposes" (Bird, 1956). In other words, is the primary purpose of the community college transfer program to approximate or even to duplicate the university lower division in content, methodology, and background and preparation of faculty, or should it prepare students satisfactorily, by whatever means, to undertake upper-division work? If the latter, community colleges should have full freedom to develop their own curricula, create methodologies, and establish standards, constrained externally only by regional accreditation requirements.

For students, the basic question ought to be: Am I prepared to handle upper-division courses? Can I compete in my major field with university students?

With a few notable exceptions, this issue has so far been resolved through a compromise allowing community colleges to develop appropriate courses within prescribed limits but rarely distinguishing between course and curriculum. Too frequently, the courses developed reflect the needs, personal and professional, of individual instructors. And too little attention is given in statewide documents to the direct relationship of these courses to curriculum requirements for the upper division and specifically for major field standing.

To this issue Henderson (1970) adds the dimension of institutional independence in the absolute sense. He observes that the associate degree is still part of the baccalaureate but shortly will be on its own and that upper-division requirements, whether baccalaureate, three-year master's, or whatever, should stand on their own with the associate degree simply a foundation for upper-level work.

Thus, the associate degree is rapidly becoming the basic transfer instrument. Even this plan, however, is not problem free.

For example, many associate-degree programs, while having important intrinsic values, may lack useful preparation for specific major fields, particularly professional fields. Another objection is that if associate degrees represent completion of all general education requirements for the baccalaureate, more than the current period will be required for it. Community college faculties would undoubtedly want to make sure that all dimensions of lower-division work are completed under their supervision. Such an extension of degree-completion time is in opposition to the current trend toward acceleration. Arbitrary separation of the general education portion and special features of the B.A. reverses the present emphasis on greater flexibility. In addition, establishing the associate degree as an absolute transfer requirement encourages senior institutions to require special admission to baccalaureate-degree programs. Such permission could be tantamount to reapplication. I discuss this situation fully later on.

While recognition of the associate degree as the sole transfer instrument has merit, it thus also has formidable drawbacks. I describe examples of such recognition and attempts to resolve some of the problems in Chapter Nine.

PART II

THE ARTICULATION SCENE

Articulation agreements that may increase the flexibility and improve the efficiency of two-year/four-year college–university transfer are rapidly being reached across the country. Led by Florida in 1965, Georgia in 1968, and now Illinois and Oklahoma, the trend is toward statewide plans that have as bases the acceptance of associate degrees or as in the case of Georgia a core curriculum. Invariably these agreements attempt to protect the integrity of both the two-year and four-year institution and establish communication among the segments.

A discussion of articulation models is presented in this chapter according to the following typology of articulation styles.

Three styles of articulation agreements are identifiable in the fifty states. Although they overlap in many details, each has distinguishing features. Under the first two styles are two different plans or systems, with subsets occurring under the second style. More than one articulation style is found in several states named in the outline and described in the first section of each chapter, notably in California, Michigan, and Texas.

In several states, articulation policies have been developed as statewide formal agreements, but in only one, Illinois, has a plan been mandated by legislation. In other states, articulation agreements have been defined primarily under the leadership of a state governmental agency or an institutional system that includes or is composed exclusively of community colleges. A third model, found in California and Michigan, emphasizes agreements developed on a voluntary basis among groups of institutions.

Reports of states identified in the typology will be presented in some detail (Chapters Four, Five and Six) following a discussion of approaches to systematizing articulation. Chapter Seven offers vignettes of all other states and the District of Columbia.

Information used in the presentations was gathered through correspondence and interviews with educators in all sections of the country. Commentary was provided by many individuals—state officials, university and senior college directors of admission, registrars, community college administrators, and counselors.

Differences among the three articulation styles are a matter of degree rather than kind. Statewide conferences are prominent in the methodology of decision-making in all states. The composition of conferences and how each is organized and coordinated are discriminating characteristics. Governance patterns of higher education heavily influence the development of a particular style.

References in Chapters Four through Seven may be found at the end of each state discussion. References in Chapter Eight are situated at the end of the chapter.

 4

Formal and Legal
Policies

The distinguishing characteristics of the formal agreement and legally based styles, first developed in Florida (1965) and later in Georgia (1968), Texas (1968), and Illinois (1972), are those of timing and breadth of contribution from the various levels of education. In these four states, all segments entered discussions at an early point and continued as task forces under the aegis of a state body. They included the State Board of Education in Florida; the University Board of Regents, which includes two-year colleges, in Georgia; the Coordinating Commission on higher education in Texas, where the core curriculum is limited to public junior colleges; and the Joint Council on Higher Education in Illinois. Illinois is the only state where the formal articulation agreement is mandated by law through sections 102–111 found in the Junior College Act of 1965.

Florida Formal Agreement Plan

Florida was the first state to develop and implement a statewide transfer agreement on general education requirements. A special committee for articulation activities, organized in 1957 and reconstituted in 1966, gave it impetus and direction. Articulation problems were identified and task-force committees organized in various subject areas. Statewide conferences were preceded by a statement on expected requirements of lower-division courses. The Professional Committee gave attention to such matters as calendars, student organizations, and articulation problems in general.

In 1965 the State Board of Education approved an articulation agreement that guaranteed junior college transfers acceptance by the state universities as juniors. The state board approved a new agreement in April 1971, which encompasses the earlier one and sets forth a number of new policies designed to facilitate transfer from the community colleges to the universities.

The 1971 agreement also established an official Articulation Coordinating Committee comprised of three representatives from the community college and three from the state university systems to recommend specific areas of agreement between community colleges and state universities; set forth criteria for awarding of the associate in arts degree; define the associate in arts degree as a component of a baccalaureate degree; provide for a continuous evaluation and review of programs, policies, procedures, and relationships affecting transfer; and recommend such revisions as are needed to promote the success and general well-being of the transfer student. The committee has established special task forces to attack such problems as the need for a common community college transcript form, a common definition of occupational courses, a policy for credit earned by examination, and the need for a common calendar. Prior to the formation of the committee, the two systems agreed upon principles for developing a common course numbering system in which private colleges may participate.

The articulation pact, approved in 1965 and reconfirmed in 1971, is based on the understanding that the transfer should be accomplished without roadblocks and that institutional integrity is of crucial importance. Education is recognized as a continuous process even though handled in separate administrative units. The community college and state university systems believe that the two structures must be meshed so that the students have a maximum opportunity to achieve their educational goals with a minimum of administrative and procedural complications.

Among the supporting policies are the following:

General Education. The provisions of the general education agreement of 1959 reaffirmed that junior college transfers should be considered as having met the general education requirements of the receiving senior institution if the junior college has certified that the student has completed the lower-division general education requirements of the junior college. This policy should apply to all junior college transfers, both graduates and nongraduates.

Associate in Arts Degree. At the core of agreement between the community colleges and the Florida state university system is the mutual acceptance of the nature and purpose of the associate in arts degree. This degree, which is the basic transfer degree of Florida junior colleges and the primary basis for admission of transfer students to upper-division study in a state university, shall be awarded when the following requirements have been met, according to the articulation agreement:

Completion of sixty semester hours (ninety quarter hours) of academic work exclusive of occupational courses and basic required physical-education courses.

Completion of an approved general education program of not fewer than thirty-six semester hours (fifty-four quarter hours).

Achievement of a grade point average of not less than 2.0 in all courses attempted and in all courses taken at the junior college awarding the degree, provided that only the final grade received in courses repeated by the student shall be used in computing this average. The grade of D will be accepted for transfer (provided the overall grade average does not drop below the prescribed 2.0 level), and will count towards the baccalaureate in the same way as D grades obtained by students enrolled in the lower division of state universities; that is, credits in courses transferred with D grades will count towards the credits required for the baccalaureate. However, it is at the discretion of the department or college of the university offering the major as to whether courses with D grades in the major may satisfy requirements in the major field.

Admission to Upper Level. Students receiving the associate in arts degree will be admitted to junior standing within the university system. The specific university that accepts the student will be determined by the preference of the student, by the program of major concentration, and by space available within the specific institution. If because of space or fiscal limitations any state university must select from among qualified junior college graduates, its criteria for selection shall be reported to the new coordinating committee.

Baccalaureate Degree. The baccalaureate degree in all state universities shall be awarded in recognition of lower-division (freshman-sophomore) combined with upper-division (junior and senior) work. The general education requirement of the baccalaureate degree shall be the sole responsibility of the institution awarding the associate in arts degree in accordance with the general education agreement of 1959. If a student has not completed an approved general education program in a junior college prior to his transfer to a state university, the general education requirement shall become the responsibility of the university.

Introductory Courses. Lower-division programs in all state institutions enrolling freshmen and sophomores may offer introductory courses that permit the student to explore the principal professional specializations that can be pursued at the baccalaureate level. These introductory courses shall be adequate in content to be fully counted toward the baccalaureate degree for students continuing in such a professional field of specialization. However the determination of the major course requirements for a baccalaureate degree, including courses in the major taken in the lower division, shall be the responsibility of the state university awarding the degree.

Catalog as Contract. Each state university shall include in its official catalog of undergraduate courses a section stating all lower-division prerequisite requirements for each upper-division specialization or major program. The sections of the catalog may also list additional recommended courses, but there shall be no ambiguity between statements of requirements for all students for admission to upper-division work, on the one hand, and prerequisites and other requirements for admission to a major program on the other. All requirements for admission to a university, college, or program should be set forth wth precision and clarity.

Experimental Programs. Experimental programs in all institutions are encouraged. A junior college and a university wishing to engage in a joint program that varies from the existing transfer policy shall report such a program to the coordinating committee before implementation and shall keep the committee informed of the progress and outcome of such experimentation. Proposed experimental programs that would have systemwide implication or would affect transfer to more than one institution must be approved by the coordinating committee prior to implementation. All experimental programs shall be reported in writing to the coordinating committee including the purpose, the design, the participants, the duration, and the results of the experiment. The final report shall be submitted not later than six months following the termination date of the experiment.

Coordinating Committee. A junior college–university coordinating committee will be established to review and evaluate current articulation policies and formulate additional policies as needed. The coordinating committee shall be composed of seven members, three of whom shall be appointed by the director of the division of community colleges, three by the chancellor of the state university system, and one by the commissioner of education. This committee shall have a continuous responsibility for junior college–university relationships and shall perform the following functions, according to the articulation agreement:

Authorize professional committees or task forces consisting of representatives from both levels of higher education to facilitate articulation in subject areas.

Conduct a continuing review of the provisions of this agreement.

Review individual cases or appeals from students who have encountered difficulties in transferring from a community college to a university. Decisions reached by the coordinating committee will be advisory to the institutions concerned.

Make recommendations for the resolution of individual issues and for policy or procedural changes that would improve junior college–university articulation systemwide.

Establish the priority to be given research conducted cooperatively by the division of community colleges and the division of universities in conjunction with individual institutions. Such cooperative research will be encouraged and conducted in areas such as admissions, grading practices, curriculum design, and follow-up of transfer students. Systemwide follow-up studies should be conducted and results of these studies will be made available to all institutions at both levels for use in evaluating current policies, programs, and procedures.

Develop procedures to improve community college–state university articulation by exploring fully specific issues such as academic record forms, general education requirements, unit of credit, course numbering systems, grading systems, calendars, and credit by examination.

Relationships with High Schools. While little attention has been given to formal agreements regarding articulation with high schools, most community colleges work closely with the ones within their district. Seniors are encouraged to visit community college campuses; arrangements are made in several community colleges for seniors to begin their college work while still completing high school; counselors are employed for summer work in the community college; occupational information is made available to students in the middle schools and junior high as well as in senior high.

Conflicts between universities and community colleges remain, especially in the area of teacher education. The problem of defining academic courses and which courses should be taught in the community college and the university still exists. Other issues to be clarified include the need to develop a common calendar, a new definition of general education, and a clarification of what is meant by vocational or occupational courses. Limitations in facilities and faculty have made it necessary to establish quotas at public universities on the admission of certain undergraduate programs. This affects transfer student members.

In summary, the division of community colleges, the state university system, and all institutions involved are committed to find mutually satisfactory solutions to articulation problems and issues.

Undergraduate Degree Program Requirements, 1971–1972 University Bulletin. Boca Raton: The Office of Academic Affairs, Florida Atlantic University, September 1971.

"Articulation Agreement Between the State Universities and Public Junior Colleges of Florida." Tallahassee, Florida: State Department of Education, March 1971.

Georgia Core Curriculum Formula

Junior colleges, senior colleges, and universities are units of the university system of Georgia—a unified statewide system of higher education. Through the joint efforts of a state committee on transfer credit and other academic committees, a core curriculum was approved in January 1967 and made effective in the fall quarter of 1968. All institutions had approved core curriculum plans by the 1969 fall term.

The core curriculum (ninety quarter hours in four areas of study—twenty each in humanities, mathematics and the natural sciences, and social sciences, and thirty hours in the major field) was approved in 1967 to aid student progress through the university system. The statement recognizes the importance of institutional responsibility to develop prescribed curricula and to innovate teaching techniques. It gives latitude to indecisive students and permits career decisions during their junior college years. The core curriculum provides areas of study rather than specific courses, giving the institution latitude in developing its own curriculum.

All junior college registrars are provided with the *Core Curriculum Registrar's Handbook,* which enables them to evaluate student transcripts in terms of the approved core curriculum.

Specific policies make the following stipulations:

If only a fractional part is completed at the initial institution,

the receiving institution shall give full credit for those hours
taken and determine which courses must be taken to satisfy requirement up to the ninety-hour core-total requirement. This
is not to exceed the total number of twenty hours required in
each of the first three areas of the core and the thirty hours
required in the major field. A transfer student should be able
to graduate with the same total of credit hours as a native
student.

Proficiency examinations in any of the core curriculum
courses, when successfully passed at a sending institution (for
course credit or exemption of courses), will be honored by the
receiving institution.

Courses in the behavioral sciences that have laboratories
may be considered in either the mathematics-natural science
area (Two) or the social science area (Three). For a behavioral
science course to be considered as satisfying the requirements
under Area Two, the course must have a laboratory period or
periods as integral components, and be so described in the
catalogue of the institution wishing to use the course in this
way. The use of a behavioral science course in Area Two
would not alter in any way the requirement of a "ten-hour
sequence of laboratory courses in the biological or physical
sciences" or the requirement that mathematics be a required
subject for all students.

Foreign languages may be included in the humanities
area (One). If they are not included in this area, all students
in arts and sciences or any other fields requiring a foreign
language for the baccalaureate degree should use courses in
the major or related area Four to fulfill the language requirement.

In all courses requiring a laboratory in Area Two, the
content and the length of the laboratory periods shall be
determined by each institution, which determination shall be
honored by a receiving institution.

It is recognized that certain programs at four-year
institutions require specialized courses at the junior college
level, and students should be so counseled.

Nothing in the core should be construed to mean that

any specific course is required. Demonstrated achievement in the core area, as determined by the institution where the core or the fractional part thereof is taken, shall be the intent of this core curriculum.

Changes in any institution's core curriculum will be considered only in the fall quarter and must be approved by the transfer of credit committee and the University System Advisory Council of Presidents.

While the core curriculum has substantially solved transfer problems, the following issues remain: transfer of D grades, complete faculty acceptance of the core curriculum concept, and difficulty in some highly specialized programs of accomplishing the sixty-hour core general education in the first two years.

The core curriculum, with some revising, will undoubtedly continue to operate throughout the state system of twenty-seven public two- and four-year institutions.

"The Core Curriculum." Atlanta: The University System of Georgia. April 1970.

Texas Modified Core Curriculum

With the creation of the Coordinating Commission on Higher Education in September 1965, all Texas institutions of higher education (including the forty-four community colleges) were placed under a common coordinating agency. Under the direction of this board, a master plan, *Challenge for Excellence: A Blueprint for Progress in Higher Education,* was produced and a *Core Curriculum for Public Junior Colleges in Texas* was adopted.

Historically, junior-senior college articulation agreements were negotiated between institutions. With modifications, notably in the core curriculum, this voluntary system is favored over state intervention. The following principles of articulation are found in the core curriculum document:

The phrase *freely transferable,* used in the enabling legislation, is interpreted to signify that course credits that are

freely transferable must apply toward degree requirements at
the senior colleges.

Since baccalaureate-degree requirements vary widely,
the core curriculum should also vary from major to major.

The coordinating board clearly states that senior colleges should be allowed to innovate or experiment with curricula, course content, and teaching methods, and that junior
colleges should be allowed to offer additional courses beyond
those listed.

Admission policies and procedures are generally standard in
Texas public senior colleges and universities. University-wide authority for granting transfer credit is given to the director of admissions, while department chairmen usually make degree-requirement
and course-equivalency determinations.

This general policy is made specific in guidelines in a document on the core curriculum:

Each Texas public senior college or university shall
accept credits earned by any student transferring from an
accredited Texas public junior college, provided such credits
are within the core curriculum of the student's declared major
field.

The senior college or university shall grant the student
full value toward degree requirements as stated in the catalog
of the senior institution and as they apply to the student's declared major.

The following are other provisions of the core curriculum
pertaining to the transferability of community college credits:

Inasmuch as the core curriculum necessarily depends
on the student's major, he is required to declare his major
field no later than the end of his first year of attendance at the
junior college and on request for admission by transfer to a
senior institution.

The student shall not be required to complete the
entire core curriculum for it to be valid and freely transferable,

but any subitem shall also be freely transferable, provided such item was completed prior to original registration in the senior institution.

The senior institution shall give any student transferring to it from a junior college the same choice in the catalog degree requirements as the student would have had if his dates of attendance at the senior institution had been the same as his dates of attendance at the junior college.

The core curriculum places no limitations on the admission of a student transferring from a junior college or any other senior institution, but it does require the senior institution to evaluate transferred credits of admissible transfer students on the same basis as if the work had been taken at the senior institution. Courses having no university equivalent are given elective credit in a particular area. If a junior college course transfers as equivalent to an advanced course (junior or senior level), the credit is denoted *unadvanced*. Evaluated equivalent courses required for a degree must be applied toward it.

Each junior college shall clearly identify on a student's transcript those courses that are terminal in nature or are so limited as to make them not generally acceptable as credit toward a bachelor's degree. It shall be the responsibility of the junior college to fully advise students of the limitations of transferring such courses for application to a bachelor's degree.

Concerning credits earned by a student in a junior college, no senior institution shall be required to accept by transfer or toward a degree more than sixty-six semester credit hours, or one-half the degree requirements if these constitute less than sixty-six hours. In addition to the courses listed in the core curriculum, the senior institutions may count additional lower-division courses that are generally acceptable in the student's major to give the total of sixty-six hours, or one-half the degree requirements if these constitute less than sixty-six hours. Although no senior institution is required by this policy to accept more than sixty-six hours, the senior institution may accept additional hours under provisions allowable by accreditation standards of the Association of Texas Colleges and Universities.

The senior college shall recognize credits earned by advanced standing examination in the junior college, but such advanced standing credit shall be a part of the core curriculum and shall not serve to extend or enlarge the number of credits transferable.

Senior institutions do not uniformly agree on the lower-division placement of certain courses. Junior colleges are occasionally denied transfer credit for courses they consistently offer in lower division. Major changes in curriculum are sometimes made by senior colleges without advance announcement to junior college administrators.

The University of Texas at Austin publishes annually a detailed booklet, *College Transfers to Undergraduate Divisions.* Much of this pamphlet is devoted to answering questions typically asked by transfers.

The Coordinating Commission on Higher Education and the Association of Texas Colleges and Universities intend to review regularly their policies on the core curriculum, adding curricula in such fields as agriculture, education, and the fine arts when developed by advisory groups.

"Core Curriculum for Public Junior Colleges in Texas." (a policy adopted by the Coordinating Board, Texas College and University System), Austin: September 1968.

Illinois Legally Based Plan

Adoption in 1964 of the master plan for higher education in Illinois and subsequent legislation establishing junior colleges as institutions of higher education set the stage for a rapid resurgence of junior college education. Guided by the Illinois Junior College Board, the state system of forty-seven comprehensive institutions, heavily supported by the state, now covers approximately 80 percent of the state.

A statement in the master plan provided the legal base upon which the Illinois Articulation Plan was developed: The Board of Higher Education continues to encourage higher education groups, particularly the Illinois Junior College Board and the Committee on Cooperation of the Illinois Conference on Higher Education, to develop organizational machinery and policies to stimulate closer articulation between junior colleges and the senior institutions in the State.

Sections 102-111 of the Illinois Junior College Act passed by the general assembly in 1965 include the development of articulation procedures as a responsibility of the Illinois Junior College Board: The state board in cooperation with the four-year colleges is empowered to develop articulation procedures to the end that maximum freedom of transfer among junior colleges and between junior colleges and degree-granting institutions be available, and consistent with minimum admission policies established by the Board of Higher Education (Darnes, 1972).

The Council on Articulation of the Conference on Higher Education was created in 1966, and a statewide meeting on articulation was held in April. Committees were created to study the transfer of students between institutions of higher education in Illinois.

While there is still no common program or uniform acceptance of transfer credit, the Illinois Joint Council on Higher Education, composed of the chief executives of the eight public universities, has agreed to accept credits "without validation" from new junior colleges for a five-year period or until accreditation has been achieved. References to these and other guidelines will be made later in this chapter in reviewing the final reports of the Articulation Study Committee to the Illinois Board of Higher Education (IBHE). The report was accepted by the IBHE and its recommendations adopted on June 1, 1971. Subsequently a new Articulation Advisory Committee was appointed in accordance with the Study Committee's recommendation. Prior to the first meeting of the committee, it was abolished by the IBHE staff. This report however serves as the most current representative analysis of junior-senior college articulation in Illinois.

The Articulation Committee functions were subsumed under a Collegiate Common Market Task Force in October, 1971. This task force is integral to Phase Three of the Statewide Master Plan.

From junior to senior college is not the dominant transfer pattern in Illinois. Community colleges receive as many transfer students as senior institutions. A significant percentage of these are reverse transfers, returning after unsuccessful attempts from universities. About one-quarter of all transfers to senior institutions are from other states (Illinois Council on Articulation, 1971). Over 50 percent of all new freshmen enrolled in Illinois higher education attend public community colleges (Illinois Junior College Board, 1971).

The philosophy supporting two-year university articulation policies is provided in the Master Plan, Phases One, Two, and Three. It indicates that lower-division education in the future rests largely in the two-year college—that transfer preference should be given to community college graduates over all other students at Illinois state colleges and universities. There follow guidelines adopted June 1, 1972, by the Board of Higher Education and ratified by most public and private institutions:

> Junior and senior institutions should cooperate in developing mutually agreed upon transfer programs to replace the senior institution practice of scrutinizing course content.
>
> Once agreement is reached, senior institutions in cooperation with junior colleges should produce documentary evidence of such agreements.
>
> These agreements should include the satisfaction of lower-division general education graduation requirements for associate degree holders who continue in the same major field.
>
> Transfer courses not applicable or useful as general education credit should be applied toward the baccalaureate degree either as elective credit, major core requirements, or in similarly useful ways for those transfer students who continue in the same major field.

In addition, at the same time the Articulation Study Committee recommended and the Board of Higher Education adopted the following guidelines for consideration of students enrolled in occupational programs:

> Institutions should recognize their responsibility to provide advanced educational opportunity to those individuals

who possess rising aspirations and who have demonstrated interest and ability in occupational or technical junior college programs as well as to those enrolled in baccalaureate-oriented programs.

Senior institutions should be encouraged to design a variety of capstone programs that build on competencies gained in junior college technical and occupational programs and/or work experience.

Senior institutions should consider each non-baccalaureate-oriented applicant as an individual in making assessments for admission and transfer of credit, and should, therefore, consider recommendations of junior college staff and other appropriate individuals in evaluating non-baccalaureate-oriented transfers.

Senior institutions should grant full credit for the general education courses of non-baccalaureate-oriented transfer students enrolled in occupational programs provided the courses meet the general education objectives required for the baccalaureate degree.

Credit earned in technical courses in non-baccalaureate programs should be applied in terms of their equivalence to baccalaureate courses in either the major field or electives when transferred to a baccalaureate-degree program.

The Articulation Study Committee also recommended to the Board of Education at the same time guidelines for setting priorities for the admission of transfer students into baccalaureate-degree programs of universities:

First preference should be given to applicants who have completed an associate degree in baccalaureate-oriented programs, to those who have completed equivalent demonstrated achievement in baccalaureate-oriented programs, and to those who seek admission to highly specialized programs that cannot be pursued profitably at their present institutions. If all applicants cannot be accepted in these categories, selection should be made on the basis of demonstrated achievement and other criteria set by the institution.

Second preference should be given to those applicants who have completed at least one but less than two years of credit in a baccalaureate-oriented program. If all applicants in this category cannot be accepted, selection should be made on the basis of demonstrated achievement and other criteria set by the institution.

If spaces remain, other applicants who have completed less than one year of credit in a baccalaureate-oriented program should be considered for admission on the basis of demonstrated achievement and other criteria set by the institution.

In February 1972, Northern Illinois University announced a new transfer policy with an associate degree in a college-parallel program effective fall term 1972. An individual transferring from an Illinois public community or junior college to Northern Illinois University who possesses the following qualifications will be admitted to the university with junior class standing; further, he will have satisfactorily met the university's general education requirements: an associate degree from the college in a baccalaureate-oriented program consisting of at last sixty semester hours of credit; at least a 2.0 (based on a 4.0 scale) cumulative grade point average as determined according to the community or junior college grading policy. Students are advised for graduation and teacher-education requirements to make up deficiencies (below c grades) in the courses equivalent to Speech 100 (fundamentals of speech) and English 103 (rhetoric and composition) prior to transfer.

There are however some credit problems caused by junior college practices. Some junior colleges still do not specify general education requirements for all baccalaureate-oriented two-year programs, although this is being corrected by a uniform general education requirement at all community colleges. Content of some junior college courses is difficult to determine, and this becomes a particular deterrent in transfer to specific fields. Some junior colleges do not specify whether their courses are designed for transfer or for vocational and technical students, and this makes it difficult for the director of admissions to know whether these courses actually prepare the student for university degree work. In other cases, junior colleges fail to inform students that many of their vocational-technical courses are not designed for transfer. Others report only passing grades or have no specific definition of a transfer student.

Major growth at the state colleges and universities in Illinois is destined to be in the upper-division and graduate programs, particularly since the Illinois Board of Higher Education master plan specifies that lower-division enrollments be held to current levels on all public state university campuses (except the Chicago Circle campus of the University of Illinois and the Edwardsville campus of Southern Illinois University). Admission policies are therefore being planned to encourage transfer at the junior level. This is intended to increase the bachelor degrees produced by the university system and make more effective use of the state facilities.

Part of the master plan has resulted in the establishment of two upper-division and first-year graduate universities, one beginning in the fall of 1970 and the other in the fall of 1971. These institutions are being designed especially to accept junior college graduates, particularly majors in the humanities, social science, business and commerce, and education.

Phase Three of the master plan for higher education emphasizes the establishment of an integrated system of higher education in Illinois. Special emphasis is given to the integrated planning of professional and graduate programs, institutional size in capacity, a possible library and learning resources network, a possible state computer network, and expanded community services and continuing education. Implementation of the adopted guidelines by the Board of Higher Education will complete the initial planning and delivery system for efficient higher education in Illinois.

Illinois Board of Higher Education. *Final Report of the Articulation Study Committee.* June 1971.

Illinois Board of Higher Education. *Board Meeting Minutes and Executive Director's Report.* University of Illinois at Chicago Circle, Chicago Circle Center. July 1971.

Illinois Council on Articulation. *Performance of Transfer Students Within Illinois Institutions of Higher Education,* November 1971.

Illinois Junior College Board. *Report of Selected Data and Characteristics of Illinois Public Junior Colleges,* 1970–1971, Spring 1971.

Illinois Junior College Board. *Comprehensive Community College Bulletin,* July 1971.

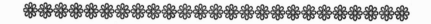

State System Policies

In the several states illustrating this type, the state body responsible for community college education tends to be a controlling rather than a coordinating agency. While in every case all levels of education contributed to the formation of statewide agreements, heavy responsibility for policy development and implementation, if a state government agency, is held by that agency. An example of this would be the State Regents for Higher Education and the State Board of Higher Education in Oklahoma. If it is an institutional system, such policy development and implementation is centered in the institutional board as in the University Board of Regents in Hawaii or the Board of Trustees, the University of Kentucky. Either system tends to be relatively inflexible.

State Agency

North Carolina Guidelines. All two-year post-high school institutions in North Carolina are supervised by the State Board of Education. A Community College Advisory Council advises the state board on policy matters, including articulation. Each school, whether community college (fifteen of them in all), technical institute (forty-one), or contracted technical institute (fifteen), has a local Board of Trustees. These changes from a dual state-agency system were included in the 1963 Higher Education Act.

Two years later, a Joint Committee on College Transfer Students was appointed. Resembling the California and New Jersey plans, an intricate system of articulation study committees involving about 1000 educators has evolved. Regular articulation conferences are held. Guidelines were published in 1967 for admissions, biological sciences, English, foreign languages, humanities, mathematics, physical sciences, and social science. The Joint Committee on College Transfer Students is a standing committee of the North Carolina Association of Colleges and Universities.

The joint committee has developed a reference manual, *Policies of Senior Colleges and Universities Concerning Transfer Students from Two-Year Colleges in North Carolina.* This volume, prepared in loose-leaf binding, will be updated annually.

A publication developed by Darrell H. Nicholson, registrar of Chowan College, called *A Step Ahead* (1971), is a significant contribution. Nicholson has included in the volume official transfer policies of almost 150 senior colleges and universities accredited by the Southern Association of Colleges and Schools. The publication is intended to serve as a ready reference for the counselor or two-year college student (prospective or otherwise) on transfer.

A superboard for all of higher education has recently been created in North Carolina. The new governing board has been given broad powers over the state's public universities and senior colleges. "The board is authorized to approve all new degree programs, dismantle unproductive and unnecessary old ones, set budget priorities, and name the chancellors of all campuses. With such powers, Governor Scott said in a message to the lawmakers, the board should be able 'to remove higher education from the political thicket' " (*The Chronicle of Higher Education,* Nov. 8, 1971).

A bachelor of technology degree was approved in August 1969 at the University of North Carolina at Charlotte. Students holding the associate in applied science degree in appropriate engineering technologies may transfer.

In 1970 a bachelor of technology degree was approved at

Appalachian State University with options in business and engineering technologies. Students holding the associate in applied science degree in appropriate fields may transfer as full juniors. These programs are designed to prepare technical and vocational instructors for two-year institutions.

Western Carolina University is in the process of establishing admission policies for transfer students from two-year institutions with course credits applied to existing B.A. or B.S. degree programs. Technical courses are validated by each department.

In 1971 Mars Hill College began offering a bachelor of science degree in nursing and other allied health programs. Students may fulfill these degree requirements in any one of three ways. They may first attend an accredited two-year institution to receive their professional preparation. After receiving their two-year degree and certification in one of the allied health professions, they would be eligible to attend Mars Hill College and pursue the allied health curriculum. Upon completion of the curriculum, students would be awarded the bachelor of science degree with a major in their area of certification (nursing, medical records, and so on). Another option would be the reverse of the procedures described above. A final option open to students would be to attend Mars Hill College for one year, proceed to the two-year institution for professional preparation and certification, and return to Mars Hill for a final year of upper-level work.

Sixteen technical institutes are offering general education curricula with college transfer options. This is a cooperative effort between an institution in the system of community colleges and a senior college or university, private and public. Credits earned in these programs are accepted by senior colleges and universities.

For the fall term 1971, the thirteen community colleges enrolled three times as many students in vocational and technical education as in transfer education.

Articulation guidelines for transfer admission adopted by the Board of Higher Education in December 1970 include the following:

Junior college students who are ineligible to enter a four-year institution at the freshman level because of poor high school records should not be denied admission as transfer students on these grounds. It is recommended that the original college consider use of standardized tests, given at the end of the third or beginning of the fourth semester or sixth quarter, to guide those students seeking entrance to another institution.

Aptitude and achievement test scores may be useful to counselors as supplementary information in assisting junior college students to make wise decisions about transfer. However, applicants who qualify for transfer on the basis of their grades in junior college should not be denied admission solely on the basis of test scores.

Except in unusual circumstances, students entering a two-year institution should complete their program at that same school.

Senior colleges should consider all grades earned by the prospective transfer. Acceptance or rejection of courses passed with a grade of D should be at the discretion of the receiving institution. Students from junior or senior colleges should be able to transfer at least one-half the hours required for graduation.

Students with satisfactory records seeking to transfer from institutions not accredited should be accepted provisionally by the senior institution pending satisfactory completion of at least one full semester's work.

For senior institutions offering the baccalaureate in technology degree: (1) Except in unusual circumstances students entering the four-year institution should hold the associate in applied science degree in appropriate areas of technical specialization. (2) Students holding A.A.-A.S. degrees in appropriate areas of technical specialization and meeting other institutional entrance requirements should be admitted to the program as junior-year students. (3) Technical graduates seeking to transfer from nonaccredited institutions should be accepted provisionally by the senior institution pending satisfactory completion of at least one full quarter or semester of course work, provided they meet other institutional entrance requirements.

For all institutions, courses taken in a technical program

may be transferred to a college or university upon validation of applicable course work through normal procedures of the receiving institution.

Some emerging areas of difficulty include the transfer of technical courses, high school or substandard college-level courses, and courses normally taught in the upper division. It is difficult to draw a definite line between college-parallel and technical courses. A few two-year colleges offer substandard courses, award college credit, and expect that same credit to be awarded for such work at the senior-college level. Several public and private senior institutions, including Mars Hill College, the University of North Carolina at Charlotte, and Appalachian State University now accept transfer students from technical institutions. The issue of the general education requirement has been considerably alleviated through the state-wide centralized joint committee mentioned several times earlier.

Articulation issues are referred to the joint committee, which serves as a forum for discussing transfer problems. Transfer policies in allied health education are now being developed.

It is anticipated that enrollment in community colleges will continue to increase. As these institutions gain in maturity, the instructional standards will be more stabilized and the students will receive better preparation for transfer to senior institutions. The community colleges are also finding that they will have to work more closely with four-year schools in establishing programs for transfer credit.

"N. C. Superboard Created to End Classic Conflict." *The Chronicle of Higher Education*. November 8, 1971.

North Carolina Board of Higher Education. *Policies of Senior Colleges and Universities Concerning Transfer Students from Two-Year Colleges in North Carolina*. Raleigh: December 1970.

Oklahoma Agreement. Oklahoma has a dual system of public two-year colleges. The eight state-supported schools are coordinated by the Oklahoma State Regents for Higher Education, but each has a Board of Regents responsible for administration of the college. The six community junior colleges are operated by local school districts, but are coordinated at the state level by the Regents.

A Role and Scope, a study of guidelines by the state regents for the 1970s, was published in February 1970 as the forerunner of the master plan for the higher education system in the state. Among its recommendations is the creation of a statewide system of comprehensive junior colleges, combining state junior colleges, community colleges, and technical institutes into an administrative unit for each of eleven districts called junior college–technical education districts. The master plan published in July 1971 endorses this recommendation for a statewide system of comprehensive junior college–technical education by 1980, with a separate governing board for each of the service areas or regions (Oklahoma State Regents for Higher Education, 1970).

The 1971 master plan recommended that formal transfer policies should be developed by 1973 to assure that a graduate of a public two-year college in Oklahoma who has successfully completed the general education requirements for the associate degree will be eligible to transfer his work to a four-year college or university without the necessity of completing additional lower-division general education courses. This recommendation undoubtedly hastened the development of an articulation agreement adopted by the state system of junior colleges and the two state universities.

Developments in recent years have also led toward the recently announced agreement. For example, the state regents had adopted uniform admission and retention standards by type of institution. Under leadership of the state regents, institutions cooperatively developed uniform course numbering for lower-division course offerings. Two-year colleges have cooperatively approved a core program of general education requirements for the associate degree. Some four-year colleges began offering baccalaureate level occupational programs, particularly in health- and engineering-related technologies, which permit upward mobility of community college students in those fields.

The provisions of the general education agreement of 1972 refer to all state junior colleges, community junior colleges, and private junior colleges recognized by the Oklahoma State Regents for Higher Education, but only to public senior colleges and universities. The plan is similar to the Florida agreement with adaptations to fit the Oklahoma scene:

Each public institution of higher education in Oklahoma is encouraged to establish a program of general education. This basic program for students working toward a baccalaureate degree requires at least thirty-three semester hours of academic credit.

The institutions are encouraged to exchange ideas in the development and improvement of general education programs. . . . While the institutions are to work cooperatively in the development and improvement of general education programs, each institution continues to be responsible for determining the character of its own program.

At the core of any agreement to establish an efficient transfer process for junior college students is the mutual acceptance of the nature and purpose of the traditional transfer associate degrees.

After a public institution of higher learning has developed and published its program of general education, the integrity of the program will be recognized by the other public institutions in Oklahoma. Once a student has been certified by such an institution as having completed its prescribed general education program, culminated by an associate of arts or science degree, no other public institution of higher learning in Oklahoma to which he may transfer will require any further lower-division general education courses in his program.

Transfer students with associate degrees who come to senior colleges or universities with the general education pattern outlined above would have earned fifty hours of general education. They would also have in most cases the proper work to meet the teacher education general education requirements.

It is understood however that teacher education candidates might have to take additional courses in general education to meet minimum certification requirements as defined by the state; that is, health and physical education, geography, Oklahoma history, or similar requirements of other professional fields. . . .

The baccalaureate degree in all Oklahoma senior-level

institutions shall be awarded in recognition of lower-division (freshman-sophomore) combined with upper-division (junior-senior) work. The lower-division general education requirement of the baccalaureate degree shall be the sole responsibility of the institution awarding the associate degree, providing the general education requirements are met.

Lower-division programs in all state institutions enrolling freshmen and sophomores may offer introductory courses that permit the student to explore the principal professional specializations that can be pursued at the baccalaureate level. These introductory courses should be adequate in content to count toward the baccalaureate degree for students continuing in such a professional field. The determination of the major-course requirements for a baccalaureate degree, including courses in the major taken in the lower division, shall be the responsibility of the institution awarding the degree. Courses classified as junior-level courses but open to sophomores at senior institutions, even though taught at a junior college, . . . should be transferable as satisfying that part of the student's requirement in the content area. Programs of comparable purpose at the senior-level institutions should have comparable and similar lower-level requirements.

Other associate degrees and certificates may be awarded by a junior college for programs having requirements different than the aforementioned degrees or a primary objective other than transfer. Acceptance of course credits for transfers from such degree or certificate programs will be evaluated by the senior-level institution on the basis of applicability of the courses to the baccalaureate program in the student's major field.

Each senior-level institution department shall list and update the requirements for each program leading to the baccalaureate degree and shall publicize these requirements for all other state institutions.

Each senior-level institution shall include in its official catalog of undergraduate courses information stating all lower-division prerequisites for each upper-division course. The sections of the catalog may also list additional recommended courses, but there shall be no ambiguity between statement of requirements for admission to upper-division work and requirements for admission to a major program. All requirements for admission to a university, college, or program must be set forth with clarity.

Each institution shall keep a complete academic record for each student. A standard form for recording the academic performance and credits of students should be considered for all state institutions.

Experimental programs in all institutions are encouraged. A junior college and a senior college or university wishing to engage in a joint specific experimental program that varies from the existing transfer policy shall report the program to the proposed articulation committee prior to implementation. The institution shall keep the committee informed of the progress and outcome of the experiment.

Students cannot transfer from an area-vocational school to a junior or senior college, not even in the same technology, since the educational programs of vocational schools are not accredited as college level. In some instances, transfer students are able to receive credit for both academic and vocational courses taken in two-year colleges by passing advanced-standing examinations. With the development of the 1972 agreement however transfer problems among institutional members of the state system are at a minimum.

It is likely that both the state-supported junior colleges and the community colleges will need to assume a greater share of responsibility for providing adult education, and counseling services for both young persons and adults. These colleges can do much to aid students in making wise vocational choices and in establishing programs of community services to improve the cultural, economic, and technical-vocational education of a postsecondary level to meet the needs of an industrialized economy.

The 1972 articulation agreement is a milestone in Oklahoma higher education.

Oklahoma State Regents for Higher Education. *Admission and Retention Policies for the Oklahoma State System of Higher Education.* Oklahoma City, November 1967.

Oklahoma State Regents for Higher Education. *Junior College Education in Oklahoma.* Oklahoma City, February 1970a.

Oklahoma State Regents for Higher Education. *Oklahoma Higher Education: A Statewide Plan for the 1970s.* Oklahoma City, July 1970b.

Oklahoma State Regents for Higher Education. *The Role and Scope of Oklahoma Higher Education.* Oklahoma City, February 1970c.

Oklahoma State Regents for Higher Education. "Articulation Agreement Between the Junior Colleges and the Senior Colleges and Universities in Oklahoma." Oklahoma City, February 1972.

Oregon System. Statutes governing the establishment of Oregon public community colleges provide that the State Board of Higher Education approve courses offered by each community college for transfer. Instructors for these courses must also be approved until the college becomes accredited by the Northwest Association of Secondary and Higher Schools. Responsibility for carrying out these provisions of the statutes have been delegated by the board to a committee representing the faculties of the four-year institutions, and chaired by the board's vice chancellor for academic affairs. With the exception of some technical courses, the courses approved for transfer parallel those offered in the lower-division programs of the four-year institutions. In most instances the transfer or nontransfer nature of a course can be determined by the course number. By agreement among the institutions concerned, certain courses or blocks of courses identified with vocational-technical numbers are transferable to specified programs in the four-year institutions. A statewide Committee on Articulation of Occupationally Oriented Programs has provided leadership and coordination in this articulation.

In 1971 the Oregon legislature codified the community college laws, including a legislative definition of the comprehensive community college. Under different legislation the legislature also assigned an articulation function to the Educational Coordinating Council.

The Oregon Community College Association has sought to maintain preplanned program transfer on a systemwide-statewide basis for four-year institutions as opposed to individual college-community college agreements. Increased transfer of technical work is an objective for a newly established liaison committee. The representatives on the new liaison committee should use the association as a communications vehicle to broaden knowledge and understanding.

The four-year institutions of the Oregon State System of Higher Education accept transfers from the thirteen Oregon community colleges, both accredited and unaccredited, on the same basis as they accept transfers from all accredited institutions— that is, evidence of eligibility to return to the last college attended and a grade-point average of 2.00 for Oregon residents. (Some institutions require a higher grade-point average for nonresident students.) A student transferring fewer than twelve term hours must also satisfy requirements for entering freshmen.

Community college courses completed after a student has earned ninety-three term hours of transferable credit may be used to satisfy course requirements of the four-year institution but are not counted toward completion of total hour requirements for the baccalaureate degree. The State System Community College Committee and a committee appointed by the presidents of the system institutions to consider specific transfer problems have recommended that this limitation be increased to 108 term hours (thereby permitting a student to complete an average of eighteen hours per term for six terms) and that the associate in arts degree be recognized as fulfilling lower-division general education requirements of the four-year institutions. These recommendations are presently under consideration by the institution faculties.

The State System Community College Committee issues an annual compilation of recommended transfer programs in the fields of study offered by the state system institutions. Students following the recommended programs will be able to complete baccalaureate degree requirements in the major they have selected without loss of credit or time. This course approval system helps to control unnecessary proliferation of courses. Community college administrators are apparently satisfied with it.

Approved curriculum areas are listed in *Oregon Community Colleges Polices and Procedures: Course and Instructor Approval.* Course applications normally include a description stating the intended coverage, class and laboratory hours per week, hours of credit, and prerequisites. Community college people are active in maintaining the basic course list.

The statewide committee on vocational-technical articulation provides opportunity for exchange of views on the problems of vocational-technical course transfer into state system institutions. The office of academic affairs, the state department of education, Oregon State University and Oregon Technical Institute (OTI), and the community colleges are represented on the committee.

Statewide meetings of state system and community college representatives are held regularly in specific subject-matter fields to consider how to articulate associate degree- and baccalaureate-degree programs. Progress has been made in three popular fields—law enforcement, nursing, and dental technology—by increasing the number of credit hours transferable from the community colleges to the state system institutions.

The student with an associate of science degree from a community college who wishes to qualify for a bachelor of technology degree from OTI can transfer, provided OTI offers a baccalaureate in his field. This has been in effect since 1967 by an agreement between the state system and community colleges. Under recent agreement between Oregon State University (OSU) and Portland Community College (PCC), OSU will accept toward degree requirements in industrial-arts teacher education a variety of technical course credits earned at PCC. These arrangements are also open to graduates of other Oregon community colleges. A number of other departments at OSU accept selected technical course credit earned in community colleges on an approved basis.

A new Council for Community College–State System Coordination, composed of representatives from the community colleges, the Community College Committee, and the State Department of Education, meets quarterly to resolve specific problems of transfer.

Concerning secondary school–community college articulation, each Oregon community college has established advisory panels of public school people to assist in improving articulation. To date the state governance agency has not played a significant role in this activity.

Efforts to facilitate transfer among the various educational units will continue. Under the guidance of the joint boards (Education, Higher Education, and Educational Coordinating Council), coordination of programs among post-high school institutions in Oregon is likely to increase. Studies are underway, in both the state system and in the community colleges, to explore alternative avenues through which learning may be sought and academic credit granted—that is, examination, work experience, independent study.

Community college services are not yet within geographical reach of all citizens and adequate financial support for state public schools at all levels continues to be a problem.

Oregon State System of Higher Education. "Transfer of Credits, Oregon State System of Higher Education—Oregon Community Colleges." Eugene, September 1971.

Virginia Plan. With the opening in 1972 of three community colleges (making twenty in all), Virginia completed Phase One of the state master plan, which recommended a two-year commuter college to serve every region in the state.

The State Council of Higher Education is the coordinating agency for all higher education. Articulation between the community college system and the four-year institutions has been greatly assisted by the state council. Each community college deals directly with secondary education within its service area, and the State Department of Community Colleges maintains liaison with the various offices of the State Department of Education.

In 1967 the Advisory Committee for Two-year/Four-year College Articulation published guidelines for the transfer of credits. To implement these guidelines, the University of Virginia published a booklet, *Admission by Transfer,* in March 1968. A joint meeting of state council staff, local board members, college presidents, and directors in the Virginia Community College System was held in the fall of that year. A general education subcommittee of the Two-year/Four-year Articulation Advisory Committee was appointed, holding its first meeting in February 1970.

Guidelines developed by the Articulation Advisory Committee of the State Council of Higher Education serve as policy on credit transfer. Guideline One of the series authorized by the State Council of Higher Education may be taken as a statement of philosophy on articulation: In order to assist students in evaluating their general progress and the appropriateness of their educational objectives, four-year institutions and two-year colleges should work jointly and establish systematic procedures to provide counselors and advisors with current and continuing information about comparable courses, curriculum changes, requirements for admission, student characteristics, student services, and performance of transfers.

Two-year college students should be encouraged to choose as early as possible the four-year institution and program into which they expect to transfer in order to plan programs that will include all lower-division requirements. Performance in the college transfer program offered by two-year colleges is the best single predictor of success in four-year institutions and should count heavily in the evaluation of transfer applicants.

Admissions standards of four-year institutions should be stated precisely, so that two-year college students may know whether they can be considered for transfer. Transfer applicants from institutions that have institutional approval from the State Council of Higher Education should be evaluated on the same basis as applicants from regionally accredited institutions.

The evaluation of transfer courses for four-year institutions should inform the individual student who has been accepted for admission how far he has advanced toward his degree objective and what residence and course requirements must still be completed.

The satisfactory completion of an appropriate two-year associate degree transfer program should normally assure upper-division standing at the time of transfer, although this does not unconditionally guarantee transfer of all credits. Achievement and aptitude testing of transfer students may be used to assist in placing the students at appropriate levels. Transfer students should be given the option of satisfying graduation requirements that were in effect at four-year institutions at the time they enrolled as freshmen, subject to the same qualifications that apply to native students.

The Two-Year/Four-Year Articulation Advisory Committee composed of representatives from public and private two-year and four-year institutions should meet at least semiannually to consider appropriate problems, suggest needed studies, and recommend to the State Council of Higher Education additional guidelines for effective articulation.

Community college transfer students are encouraged to

complete their two-year associate degrees before transferring to a senior college. Under unusual circumstances, applications of community college students will be considered by a senior college at the end of one year of community college study. In such cases the secondary school transcript and College Entrance Examination Board scores may be required of the transfer applicant.

Senior colleges and universities generally accept community college courses on an equivalency basis. Community colleges in their transfer programs offer lower-division study in general education. This policy is consistent with the state teacher-certification plan, which declares that the two lower-division years be general studies and that the upper-division years concentrate on professional education courses and subject major requirements.

University and senior college admissions officers and deans determine the appropriateness of community college transfer courses. The uniform course numbering, title, and credit system in the community colleges assists in this evaluation process. Core courses are basic to all associate-degree curricula.

Recently the Virginia Polytechnic Institute and State University established a new transfer policy for community college graduates. It clearly reveals the increasing acceptance of the community college in Virginia and the importance of effective university –community college articulation. The University of Virginia has also released a transfer statement accepting graduates from Virginia community colleges in junior standing. More than two years at the university may be necessary to complete degrees in certain curricula.

Senior colleges and universities in Virginia are taking increasing interest in the community colleges, and on the urging of the State Council on Higher Education are holding campus meetings to discuss transfer programs with community college representatives.

Virginia Community College System. *Counseling Information*. Richmond, 1971.

Institutional System

University of Hawaii Community Colleges System. Articulation policies are based on the rationale that membership in the system mandates a reciprocal and continuous liaison among all campuses regardless of degree levels. Students must however meet the program requirements of the campus to which they transfer. Responsibility for articulation at each of the eight community colleges has been assigned to the guidance and counseling divisions.

Policies and procedures dealing with admission and transfer are undergoing evaluation by the Council of Deans, Council of Provosts, and the Faculty Senates:

Students not originally admitted to Manoa (the main university campus) and Hilo may transfer after they complete a minimum of twenty-four credits of work at a community college and if they meet the general requirements.

Students originally admitted to Manoa-Hilo who begin work at a community college need not complete twenty-four credits before transferring to the university, but they must meet the grade-point average required of university students.

Students on academic suspension from Manoa-Hilo who choose to attend a community college for college transfer work must earn at that community college a minimum grade-point average of 2.0 in order to return to the university. Students who wait out the suspension semester may return to the university automatically.

Credit for a course numbered 1 through 99 (occupational and general education courses) will not be transferred from a community college to the university unless such courses meet precise needs in the student's program as designated by the appropriate Manoa-Hilo department. Should a student subsequently transfer into a program where such courses are not required, they will not count toward the degree.

Assuming the work is a part of a university program, credit and content for courses 100-299 (college-parallel courses) will transfer to Manoa-Hilo campuses, credit for the D grade will transfer, and any number of credits may be transferred from a community college to Manoa-Hilo.

Concurrent registration is allowed, since students are registered in the University of Hawaii system.

A baccalaureate degree student may meet either the

catalog requirements in effect at the time he entered the system or the requirements current at the time he transfers.

A student may fulfill his residence requirement at a community college, but to earn a baccalaureate degree he must be accepted in a program on one of the four-year campuses.

Grade points transfer automatically at the request of the individual student.

Transfer problems associated with sequential courses and preprofessional courses are being studied by a faculty group representing community colleges and four-year campuses of the university system. Some students, particularly vocational majors, feel the traditional transfer courses interfere with their primary goal (to learn a skill) or repeat high school classes. The only associate in science degree programs that are transferable to the Manoa and Hilo campuses are those taken by vocational-teacher trainees and business-education majors enrolled in the College of Education. Home-economics majors at the Manoa-Hilo campuses are asking for credit in community college courses in clothing patterns; physics majors, for credit courses in electronics. The slowdown in economy of the state has retarded the development of some community college vocational programs.

Decisions about the future direction of the University of Hawaii Community Colleges are directly related to the September 1970 policy statement of the Board of Regents on controlled growth for the university. The board is concerned about excessive growth jeopardizing the educational quality. Since the University of Hawaii Higher Education System has interlocking aspects, studies must be completed on possible maximum enrollments for each campus, the optimum growth rate to an established ceiling, the location of new colleges, and the distribution of educational programs among the colleges. Decisions affecting Manoa-Hilo and a proposed second four-year campus will cause continual reassessment of the growth rates at community colleges.

An articulation study of the entire mathematics program is currently being conducted. Another comprehensive study is in the developmental stages for model cities urban planning and health and social services.

Liberal-arts offerings on all community college campuses (to a more limited extent at Leeward) will be expanded rapidly. Clustering courses to allow a concentration of majors on particular campuses is now being considered. Professional sequences—mathematics through calculus—are not only being added on all community college campuses but are also being evaluated on a university-wide scale.

Board of Regents of the University of Hawaii. *Controlled Growth for the University of Hawaii Community Colleges.* Fall 1970.

University of Kentucky Community College System. The thirteen community colleges in Kentucky are an integral part of the university. Formerly called *university centers,* the colleges serve community needs through individual boards that advise the directors. A system-wide catalog is published annually.

Transfer courses in the community colleges parallel those offered on the university campus. They may be transferred directly to the Lexington campus of the university or to other public or private institutions. Technical courses designed to meet the requirements of two-year terminal programs offered by the community colleges are considered for university transfer on an individual basis just as courses would be from any accredited institution.

A maximum of sixty-seven semester hours of transfer course work taken in the community colleges is accepted by the state universities and colleges. At least one private four-year institution in the state will accept all credits earned in a community college including both technical and transfer course work.

Since the community colleges are a part of the University of Kentucky, the university accepts grades earned in transfer courses taken in the community colleges and includes these grades when computing the student's overall grade point average. Other state institutions record courses taken in the community colleges, but the grades earned in these courses are not used in computing the student's overall grade point average.

In the past, technical courses (T prefix in the catalogue) offered at the community colleges were not accepted by the University of Kentucky, although state universities have occasionally accepted them if they related to the student's educational goals. As for the regional state universities, this matter has ceased to be a problem as a result of action taken by the University of Kentucky. The т prefix has been dropped from all community college courses, and the regional state universities are now generally accepting these courses from Kentucky community colleges providing grades are acceptable.

The University of Kentucky has adopted a policy on the evaluation of courses offered in the University Community College System that are not offered on the Lexington campus. Essentially these courses are now evaluated on an individual basis, as they would be if they were being transferred from another institution. This change in the acceptance of community college technical courses has essentially resolved the most serious articulation problem.

Comprehensive curricula are expanding in community colleges along with other services to local districts.

University of Nevada Community College System. A state plan for community colleges in Nevada was completed in 1970. The three community colleges are developing as a division of the University of Nevada system. The principle of university course equivalency is therefore the transfer standard. Transfer credit is granted for courses equivalent to those offered in university baccalaureate curricula.

Specific transfer guidelines include the following:

The accreditation of the institution and the graded listing published in the current American Association of Collegiate Registrars and Admissions Officers' *Report of Credit Given* govern the acceptance of transfer credit: A listing— credit accepted; B listing—credit accepted after the first fifteen credits in residence are completed with a с average or above; c listing—credits accepted after the first thirty credits in residence are completed with a с average or above; E listing— credit not accepted.

Duplication of courses, excessive credit, and repeated credit are not allowed.

Credits transferred from an accredited junior college may be accepted up to a maximum of one-half the corresponding university curriculum for the degree.

Credits transferred from an accredited four-year educational institution may be accepted to within thirty semester credits of the total credits required for the degree.

Credit may be granted for lower-division courses from other institutions if they are comparable to University of Nevada upper-division courses. Such credit may be applied toward satisfying the individual college's upper-division credit or specific course requirements if approved by the dean of the college concerned.

Graduates from a one-year professional course in an accredited normal school are granted one year's credit of advanced standing in only the College of Arts and Science, Business Administration, and Education.

Transfer credit in excess of that granted for a similar university course is not allowed.

A maximum of fifteen semester hours may be earned by examination by acceptable correspondence, extension, or United States Armed Forces Institute courses. Such credit cannot be applied to the residence requirement.

Admission with advanced undergraduate standing is granted to a student transferring from another accredited college or university provided the applicant fulfills two conditions. The applicant must be in good standing at the educational institution last attended, and transcripts must be presented from each college or university attended showing a least a c average on all acceptable transfer credits. An applicant transferring to the university with less than fifteen acceptable transfer credits is required to satisfy both the transfer and freshman admission requirements.

The University Office of Admissions evaluates the transcript and records the specific course title, number, credits, and grades. The evaluation form is distributed to the office of student affairs, the academic dean, the academic adviser, the records office, and the student. The specific credit that may be applied toward satisfying degree requirements in the assigned college is determined by the adviser or dean of the college. Appeals are resolved by the admissions officer and the dean of the appropriate college.

The president of the Community College Division is represented on the Chancellor's (University of Nevada system) Articulation Committee. It is anticipated that the work of this committee, combined with the process of accreditation of community colleges and Board of Regents directives, will result in students transferring to the university in the same manner as students transferring from any other institution of higher education.

University of Nevada *Catalog,* 1972.

Wisconsin University Center System. The new University of Wisconsin system, effective in the fall of 1971, combines the former University of Wisconsin and Wisconsin State Universities. Governed by a single Board of Regents, four clusters have been established in the system: two doctoral universities at Madison and Milwaukee, eleven other universities, fourteen two-year collegiate centers in the center system, and statewide extension. The degree-granting universities accept with minimum difficulty the courses completed at the various two-year centers. Each senior institution sets its own transfer policies. The University of Wisconsin center system takes the initiative in solving transfer problems of graduates from its collegiate centers.

In cooperation with university extension, most center campuses offer adult education classes, and special workshops and institutes. Majors in certain specialized areas require transfer after one year. Most vocational-technical education is found in technical institutes.

Three technical institutes also offer academic transfer work, and therefore are community college approximations. These three "community colleges" (in Milwaukee, Madison, and Rhinelander) accommodate students who cannot meet admission requirements at other collegiate institutions and some who have had academic difficulty at universities. Others attending these schools are unsure of major fields. Vocational education at all levels still remains under the State Board of Vocational, Technical, and Adult Education (VTAE).

The Wisconsin Association of Collegiate Registrars and Admissions Officers considers articulation problems among the college institutions, and recommends changes through the respective college and university representatives. Vocational schools in the VTAE system offering college work are not eligible to belong to the association.

The Board of Regents of the two university systems approves admissions standards. Each four-year school formerly a part of the Wisconsin state university system accepts a maximum of seventy-two transfer credits. Policies vary within the university, where each college within the campus sets its own regulations. In general these have been liberalized since the *Nationwide Pilot Study on Articulation* was published two years ago (Kintzer, 1970).

On all university campuses, course-equivalency questions are handled between the office of admissions at the receiving school and the registrar at the original school. The judgment of the office of admissions is ordinarily accepted on both transfer and equivalency matters. Academic deans and department chairmen are brought in to solve the serious problems.

Credits taken in vocational-technical institutes generally are not transferable, although the University of Wisconsin-Stout accepts such credits since it specializes in training vocational teachers. If the student has a c average, d grades are acceptable. About 50% of those transferring to a university campus from a vocational-technical institute lose some credit; the average loss is approximately 8 percent. The primary reason for this inacceptability is that much vocational-technical work is nontransferable, and a second reason is the lack of applicability to the university program.

Although numerous technical colleges throughout the state would like to add college-transfer programs, it does not appear that they will be authorized to do so since most of them are located where two-year campuses of the University Center Wisconsin System already exist. It is expected that the County Teachers Colleges will shortly be discontinued.

Arizona Institutional System. An independent state board for junior colleges in Arizona was established in 1960. The law allows a county or combination of contiguous counties to organize a district. The state board controls curriculum and the local (county) boards employ personnel and make their own budgets subject to state board approval.

Local county governing boards are responsible for operating

the local colleges under the general supervision of the State Board of Directors for Junior Colleges. The Higher Education Coordinating Committee meets twice yearly to discuss transfer problems. This informal voluntary group, composed of registrars, is responsible for articulation. The director for program services from the state office is a member.

Rulings on the exact number of hours accepted are made by the standing committee of the appropriate university or college. The maximum granted cannot exceed sixty-three. A transfer student may follow the degree requirements specified in university catalogs in effect when the student begins his community college career. Upper-division credit is ordinarily not allowed for courses taken at community colleges. Special cases are reviewed by the university. Systems of credit transfer to universities vary within the state.

At Northern Arizona University all transcripts submitted for evaluation of transferable credit must contain evidence of honorable dismissal, and only college-level courses carrying grades of c (2.0) or better from accredited institutions are accepted. All such credit is accepted, hour for hour, as it applies to the requirements of the currriculum at Northern Arizona University. The university does not recognize credit earned during the time a student is on suspension. Transfer credits from one or more authorized two-year colleges will be accepted up to a maximum of one-half the requirements of the curriculum pursued at Northern Arizona University; this includes credits earned at all previous colleges. These credits must carry grades of c or better and be from a nonterminal college parallel program intended for transfer toward a bachelor's degree. Courses transferred from a two-year college may be accepted as substitutes for upper-division requirements only in special cases approved by the student's academic advisor at the university.

Two-year college transfer students may follow the degree requirements in effect at the time they begin their two-year college work, provided their attendance has been continuous and normal progress has been made.

At Arizona State University credits transferred from accredited junior colleges will be accepted up to a maximum of sixty-three semester hours. Additional credit may be accepted only upon authorization of the standards committee at the student's college at Arizona State University. Junior college students planning to transfer at the end of their first or second year should plan their courses to meet the requirements of the curriculum selected. Students will be permitted to follow the degree requirements specified in the university catalog in effect at the time they began their junior college work, providing their college attendance has been continuous. Courses transferred from junior colleges will not be accepted for upper-division credit at Arizona State University.

At the University of Arizona credits transferred from accredited junior colleges will be accepted up to a maximum allowed by the university for the first two years in the corresponding university curriculum.

As new junior colleges initiate their programs in Arizona, the university undertakes accreditation procedures promptly when requested. Pending accreditation, students from such colleges may transfer and receive full credit for all courses with a grade of B or higher that are applicable to the university degree program.

Many problems have been called to the attention of the Higher Education Coordinating Committee. The junior colleges and the universities have different residence requirements. A student can, as a resident, attend the junior college in the state for one semester and then transfer to the university thinking that he is a resident, only to find out that he is not classified as such at the university. The junior colleges have an open-door policy, and as a result have many remedial courses not designed for transfer purposes. Students who have had to take remedial courses because of academic deficiencies graduate from the junior college only to find after transferring that they have less than a junior standing. The universities as a result are falsely accused of not accepting junior college credits. And no university accepts vocational credits, or credits for which there is no parallel in the university catalog. Many students lack the ability to communicate their problems to the proper authority and are often unaware of transfer regulations.

Problems that exist seem to be at departmental and major levels rather than at the level of university-wide admissions.

About 30 percent of Arizona's eleven comprehensive community college students are enrolled in occupational programs, roughly the national average. But over 90 percent of college students in Arizona attend public institutions—one of the highest percentages in the nation. It is predicted that eight out of ten Arizona lower-division students will be in two-year colleges by 1980.

Arizona Community College Board. "Report of the Ad Hoc Committee: Transfer of Community College Credits." Phoenix, January 1972.

Iowa Institutional System. A statewide system of public-area community colleges and vocational-technical schools was established in 1965 by the Iowa Sixty-First General Assembly. Vocational-technical education was made mandatory as part of area community college programs. Each district had the choice of becoming a comprehensive college. The three senior institutions in Iowa are controlled by a single Board of Regents, and this board established several Regents' Committees to deal with transfer of credits. In 1951 a Registrar's Committee on Coordination was appointed; in 1966 a second committee, the Regents' Committee on Educational Relations, was created. The latter determines policies on the transfer of credit for the three university campuses, each represented by the registrar, an academic faculty member, and someone from professional education. At the University of Iowa, an Office of Community College Affairs and a standing University Committee on Community College Relations were also established in 1966.

Articulation activities are also conducted through statewide discipline-articulation committees encompassing all institutions of higher education, including public and private two-year institutions, the three regent institutions, and the private four-year colleges and universities. Transfer student conferences are held annually on the University of Iowa campus to inform community college counselors of changing requirements and to provide them with feedback from recent transfer students.

In an effort to provide a smoothly operating state system, the University of Iowa accepts all degree-credit courses designed for transfer from accredited community colleges.

A maximum of sixty out of sixty-six semester credits is

allowed in the transfer package. Before any of the final sixty credits are taken, all of the sixty-six lower-division credits must be completed. Community college courses that satisfy university general education requirements will be credited beyond the transfer maximum.

Students transferring from a two-year college or with a combination of four-year and then two-year college work count transfer credit hours towards a degree in excess of one-half of the credit hours required for the degree. Students who have earned associate degrees will be held for sixty-two semester hours of work in the College of Liberal Arts and will have all general education graduation requirements satisfied except for foreign languages.

All course work is accepted if it is designed to transfer to a baccalaureate program. The university accepts D grades; F grades are counted in computing a grade point average. If a course is taken more than once, only the last grade is considered.

The university admissions officer determines the acceptability and decides how transfer courses may apply toward general education requirements. Applications to major requirements are determined by the specific university department. The *Iowa Counselor Guide,* published annually by the University of Iowa, names courses that will satisfy particular requirements.

All hours attempted in transfer institutions are used in computing cumulative grade point averages. A student may transfer after his freshman year. Some courses taken at community colleges are normally taught in the upper division of the university. The nature of the course taken at the freshman or sophomore level often differs from the course offered in the upper division because of prerequisites of the latter.

Technical courses do not transfer to baccalaureate programs, although some credit may be awarded through examination.

In the foreseeable future, community college districts with comprehensive programs will probably replace the present area districts and associated vocational schools.

Massachusetts Institutional System. Massachusetts was the first state to begin a community college system fully financed by the state and sponsored by a single board. Berkshire Community College in Pittsfield was the first college formed under the regional community college system in 1960. The Board of Regional Community Colleges is the policy body for the thirteen regional institutions. In lieu of a statewide transfer policy, effectiveness of transfer primarily depends on institutional relationships. Proximity is an important factor.

The University of Massachusetts at Amherst is one of the few institutions in the country that publishes a *Transfer Students' Handbook*. The university established an Office of Transfer Affairs in September 1971, which in turn formulated a State Transfer Articulation Committee. Membership includes representatives from public and private institutions. A standard form for collecting information on transfers was one of the first accomplishments of the committee.

The University of Massachusetts is the only institution committed by public policy to accept any qualified community college student who has completed the two-year transfer program with a satisfactory academic performance and who is recommended by the appropriate community college officials. This policy was accepted in 1967 by the University Board of Trustees and endorsed by the Faculty Senate in April 1972. Beginning in the fall term 1972, associate-degree graduates received full junior standing to a maximum of sixty-four units. University core requirements may be completed at regional colleges. The university accepts as transferable D grades taken from the AA degree. High school transcripts and SAT scores are no longer included in the application admission procedure. Admission of transfers is accomplished on a joint-decision basis. The person responsible for admission at the community college schedules a meeting with one of the university transfer admission counselors. Together they make the decision on each applicant.

On October 14, 1971, the Massachusetts state college system affirmed its intent to increase flexibility in the transfer of qualified students. To implement this objective, the system established guidelines and priorities:

Applicants for transfer to any college in the Massachusetts State College System will be evaluated for admission on the basis of previous college academic record.

The state colleges will accept credits of a c or better

earned in equal or comparable courses at the institutions of public higher education in the Commonwealth. (Maintenance of a c *average* does not insure transfer to a state college.)

Whenever possible degree credit will be granted for course work completed at Massachusetts institutions of public higher education. Courses that do not fit the degree program may be counted as fulfilling the open elective requirements of the four-year curriculum. The transfer student will be required to fulfill the same degree requirements as any other student.

Honors courses, programs of independent study, or Advanced Placement and College Level Examination Program (CLEP), and advanced standing credit earned at another Massachusetts institution of public higher education will be accepted at any state college.

Whenever feasible, the state colleges will not institute highly specialized courses needed for the degree program prior to the junior year.

A student must successfully complete one year as a full-time student to receive a baccalaureate degree from any state college.

The number of transfers accepted by each state college will be determined by existing vacancies in the various degree programs and the number of applicants determined eligible under the above guidelines. Among equally qualified and eligible transfer applicants, priority in admissions will be as follows: (1) First priority is given to transfer students in good standing from within the State College System. (2) Second priority is given to qualified transfer applicants from community colleges.

To implement these guidelines and priorities, state college presidents will be obliged to commit additional spaces for transfer students, instead of saving available spaces for freshmen, and to initiate joint meetings of subject-area specialists.

Some university and state college departments still question regional college ability to offer quality education, particularly in specific fields. These fears are gradually being dispelled in Massachusetts as elsewhere by satisfactory performance of transfer students.

Massachusetts State College System. "Transfer Policy for the State College System," 1971.

Missouri Institutional System. Many of the senior institutions in Missouri accept associate degrees earned by students in the twenty public community colleges without further evaluation. The four campuses of the Missouri university system approved the following policy statement in April 1971 as adapted from a recommendation issued by the Missouri Commission on Higher Education:

A student admitted to the university and holding an associate degree oriented toward the baccalaureate degree will be accepted in junior standing if he has a grade point average of c or above as validated by an accredited institution. This does not exempt the student from meeting the specialized lower-division degree requirements and the specialized requirements of departments or divisions of the university. Courses completed in the associate-degree program will be evaluated for application to specific degree requirements with the same criteria used for transfer students from other colleges and universities, from other campuses of the University of Missouri, and from other divisions of the same university campus.

A student transferring to the university without an associate degree oriented toward a baccalaureate degree will have his transcripts evaluated on a course-by-course basis.

Community college transfers receive credit for d grades at many of Missouri's colleges and universities, particularly if the student has the associate degree. It is too early to assess the effectiveness of the articulation policies. There continue to be transfer cases where loss of credits is reported and where general education requirements in senior institutions must be made up. Courses with technical designations are not acceptable in senior colleges and universities. The Junior College Section of the Missouri State Department of Education and the Missouri Commission on Higher Education are serving as monitors. These agencies jointly assess the degree and success of implementation of the current articulation policies and initiate and coordinate discussion and modification.

Central Missouri State College. *The Transfer of Credits from Junior Colleges to Senior Colleges.* (A Report of the Fifth Annual Missouri Valley Conference on Cooperation Between Junior and Senior Colleges) April 1970.

New Jersey Institutional System. This state is a newcomer to the community college movement. Although several so-called experimental junior colleges were opened in the early thirties, concerted action did not begin until late 1958 with the establishment of the Office of Community and Two-year College Education. Recommendations of a state study committee were translated into legislation: the County College Bill of 1963, which created a system of two-year comprehensive institutions under the Department of Higher Education. There are currently fourteen colleges in the state system. The Council of County Colleges is advisory to the Department Chancellor.

Phase One of the state master plan has been completed; Phase Two, including the role and function of the county colleges, was completed in the fall of 1971. An articulation conference that may become like that of California is under way. An initial blue-ribbon conference on transfer procedures, held in January 1970, resulted in the appointment of a steering committee to attack some of the problems. The conference discussed a cluster plan under which a senior college would develop an agreement with nearby two-year colleges as an alternative to the formation of statewide subject-area articulation committees.

Section One of the master plan announces ten goals of the higher-education system, several of which have particular relevance for the community college: elimination of financial barriers, more diversity and flexibility, and implementation of programs to meet community needs. It was agreed that diversity among institutions should be complemented by diversity within. A greater number of out-of-state students was recommended. Higher education in the state had tended to segregate students of differing ability levels at different institutions.

Phase Two of the New Jersey master plan for higher education outlines the roles of the various institutions and has superseded much of the previous work on transfer policies from junior to senior institutions. The master plan states the intention of working toward adapting the system of higher education to a more varied pattern of student interest and need. It also declares the intention of the state to develop a true system of education whereby relationships between institutions are flexible and transferring is easy. The master plan includes the principle that two-year college graduates of lower-division baccalaureate programs are entitled to a space in a four-year college. They are also entitled to clarification of all transfer programs and full transfer of credit.

The master plan decision on the necessity of placing two-year college graduates within the system has eliminated much of the case-by-case aspect of transfer. However procedures and operational policies differ from institution to institution within the system. For example, some will accept an entire package of general education, while others will not take all credits earned at a county college; typing, bookkeeping, and elementary algebra are frequently on the unacceptable list. Rutgers University will accept D grades in sequential courses when the student shows proficiency in advanced courses; D grades are acceptable within the various schools at Rutgers. Princeton University selects transfer candidates with strong academic records and demonstrated academic promise in specific fields, but only when the university is underpopulated. Credit hours are not counted; students are admitted as sophomore or juniors. Some four-year colleges eliminate grade point averages from two-year college transcripts. Most accept credits for advanced placement; several accept College Level Examination Program tests as advanced placement credit.

A volunteer committee, composed of the Department of Higher Education staff and representatives from public and private two- and four-year institutions, has achieved some worthwhile objectives. They have established a single application form for the community colleges and senior institutions alike, which helps to get colleges to work on basically the same timetable. For those students not accepted by an institution, a clearinghouse process staffed by community college transfer counselors and four-year college admissions counselors meet and place two-year graduates. The result is placement for all students.

The volunteer committee has also published a student handbook to New Jersey community colleges, drawn up articulation and transfer guidelines for all public institutions, and provided for a study on the academic success of transfer students in four-year programs.

The committee is attempting to solve a variety of other problems. Senior institutions for example are examining double standards, the quality of two-year county college courses. Lack of integration of specific disciplines, such as county college chemistry with senior college chemistry, is another problem. And sometimes two-year college students, attempting to meet general education requirements listed in a senior college catalog, are blocked by different requirements by the time they are ready to transfer.

Articulation is also being studied by a Task Force Committee appointed in the fall of 1971 by the New Jersey Consortium on the Community College. The Task Force submitted recommendations in May 1972 which stipulate that the associate degree should be the only general admission requirement to the four-year institutions. A subcommittee is studying the feasibility of forming upper-division colleges.

Future plans of the state groups include increasing emphasis on articulation of curricula between two- and four-year colleges and among two-year institutions. This effort not only shows a concern for transferability, but has a wider importance in elucidating and broadening offerings in New Jersey higher education.

Goals for Higher Education in New Jersey. Trenton: New Jersey Board of Higher Education. January 1970, No. 1.
"Articulation/Transfer Task Force Report." Trenton: New Jersey Consortium on the Community College, May 1972.

New York Institutional System. All thirty-eight public two-year colleges are under the overall supervision of the Board of Trustees of the State University of New York. The six agricultural and technical colleges are integral units of the State University of New York (SUNY) and are completely state funded. The community colleges have local trustees—five appointed by the local sponsors and four by the governor. Both the community colleges and the agricultural-technical colleges are comprehensive institutions.

The urban centers operate under contracts with the public two-year colleges and are designed primarily to serve economically and educationally disadvantaged students, either by preparing them for immediate employment or for the academic skills necessary to continue college. The cooperative college centers are state financed. They include cooperative efforts among public and private two- and four-year institutions to provide counseling, remedial-developmental courses, and some college-level work for these deprived students. Colleges participating in the cooperative college centers agree to admit students who have completed the center programs successfully.

Eight of the community colleges have the same sponsor and board of trustees as the City University of New York (CUNY)—the Board of Higher Education of the City of New York—and thus also have a close relationship with the city university.

The Commission for Higher Education of the State University of New York, the coordinating agency for SUNY, has legal and final responsibility for all master planning and articulation. Improvements in articulation are effected in cooperation with the State University, City University, and the Commission of Private Colleges and Universities. The president of the latter organization and the chief executives of SUNY and CUNY, called *chancellors,* serve as an advisory board to the Commissioner of Education, who is also the president of SUNY.

"Let Each Become All He Is Capable of Being" is the motto of the state university. These words express clearly the philosophy of the state university system of which the public two-year colleges are a part. To accomplish this, articulation must take place at many levels. Articulation efforts are described under the policies and procedures section.

Nearly all the community colleges operate full opportunity programs. These programs, which apply to residents of sponsorship areas, guarantee to every recent high school graduate and every veteran released during the preceeding year admission to a full-time program geared to their interest and level of achievement. The full opportunity program requires that the individual colleges submit plans that include their articulation efforts with high schools.

Some colleges have developed plans with cooperating high schools so that students are able to attend both college and high school and receive college credit prior to high school graduation. The agricultural and technical colleges provide opportunities for students from areas not served by community colleges. These colleges also offer programs for which there is a state need, but which would not be justified on the basis of need in any local area.

The urban centers and cooperative college centers provide opportunities for adults—mostly beyond high school age—who need immediate skills to get jobs or take college courses. The community colleges supervise the urban centers. Students completing urban center college adapter programs are then able to move into the supervising community colleges. Students completing the cooperative college center programs are assured a position in one of the cooperating colleges.

The 1968 State University of New York master plan assures that every qualified graduate of a two-year program can continue his education at the university. Students who complete a two-year college program successfully in New York state are generally able to move into one of the four-year colleges. Graduates of two-year university-parallel programs are generally admitted to the junior year in the four-year college and can graduate in two additional academic years. Graduates of career-oriented programs who continue their education can usually plan on spending more than two years for a baccalaureate degree, except in a few cases where capstone programs have been developed for certain areas. In order to implement the master plan recommendation to provide increased access to continuing education, the State University of New York is planning to establish four regional areas in which any community college graduate would be guaranteed admission to a public or private senior college. The most generally agreed-upon cooperation is in the use of computers and libraries. Most difficult to resolve is exchanges of students either in part-time (one term) or full-time residence. Tuition differences, residency requirements, graduation requirements, course-work distribution requirements, minimum acceptable transfer grades, parallelism of previous courses all provide stumbling blocks for some colleges. It is expected however that the plan will become fully operational by September 1974. Therefore, articulation among institutions and among faculty within those institutions should continue to focus on regions.

Universities in the SUNY system are beginning to develop policies and procedures on admissions and guidelines for course and credit acceptance (see Kintzer, *Nationwide Pilot Study on Articulation*, pp. 83–89, for developments at the State University at Buffalo).

At the present time, the City University of New York provides automatic admission of community college transfer students to the senior colleges of City University from the eight community colleges under the Board of Higher Education of the City of New York.

The Office of Two-Year Colleges has played a prominent role in the articulation process within the state university system. This office has acted to focus attention on the needs of two-year college graduates and has encouraged statewide and regional articulation conferences that brought together faculty from two-year colleges, four-year colleges, and universities. The Office of Two-Year Colleges has also issued articulation statements that have stimulated discussion among the policy-makers within the university. This process itself has been a factor in the commitment to guarantee admission to a senior college of any community college graduate by 1974.

Problems related to articulation between two- and four-year colleges include the questions of local autonomy contrasted with overall state needs; exclusivity as opposed to open access; what proportion of freshmen should be educated in two-year colleges; cost differentials between educating students living at home and in dormitories; and availability of programs to students from career-oriented programs who wish to continue their education.

It is possible that in this decade many more students will enter career-oriented rather than baccalaureate programs. What effect this will have on associate degree programs and articulation is still not clear. At the same time a number of events taking place in higher education, particularly within the state university system, should ease problems of articulation. The new Empire State College, a college without walls, will provide two-year college graduates with an opportunity to continue toward a baccalaureate degree in nontraditional ways. The success of this approach may serve existing institutions as a model for greater flexibility. The State Education Department is developing a series of examinations that will qualify individuals for a degree without having attended a traditional college class. See Chapter Nine for a description of this program.

Community College Handbook, 1969. The City University of New York, Office of Admission Services, 1969.

"Junior-Senior College Transfer Policies and Practices in New York State: A Profile." Intercollege Relations Committee, New York State Personnel and Guidance Association, 1968.

Pennsylvania Institutional System. According to the Pennsylvania *Master Plan for Higher Education,* the 174 degree-granting institutions in the state are divided into five groups: the thirteen state-owned colleges and Indiana University of Pennsylvania; the three state-related commonwealth universities (Pennsylvania State University, Temple University, and the University of Pittsburgh); the fourteen community colleges; 118 independent institutions including specialized universities, twelve junior colleges, and professional schools; and the thirty proprietary schools where at least one program has been approved for the specialized associate degree. The master plan has not been formally adopted by the state legislature, although many of its recommendations have been implemented. The powers of the State Board of Education are yet to be defined.

A statewide system of community colleges was created by the Community College Act of 1963, and it became a reality with the opening of Harrisburg Area Community College the following year. While Pennsylvania had long been recognized as a state with an imposing number of universities and colleges, most of them were privately endowed and involved high tuition and selectivity.

The five segments of the higher education system are coordinated by the Council for Higher Education of the State Board of Education. Representatives of each of the five segments meet periodically with the State Commissioner for Higher Education.

Goals of the five segments include provision in state-owned

and state-related institutions for community college transfer; limitation on graduate programs in keeping with commonwealth needs; emphasis on the feeder function of branch campuses; and general coordination of efforts to prevent overlapping of academic programs.

Penn State University—currently a twenty-campus system— is well integrated. Colleges and departments have unified faculties who also serve on the eighteen commonwealth campuses, which offer two-year programs. The Capitol campus is limited to upper-division and graduate work; the Behrend campus now offers the junior and senior years in a limited number of majors.

Most of the state colleges accept a minimum of sixty liberal arts transfer credits with a c grade or better from the community colleges. Some also accept certain credits from nontransfer programs.

It is generally accepted that all progress begins with communication between institutions and that defined articulation provides the keystone for achieving the mutual goals of all institutions in the commonwealth. Each individual attending a two-year college should have the opportunity of higher education.

An articulation conference at West Chester State College in March 1971 recommended establishing regional articulation committees to represent all institutions and the state Department of Education. These committees would be convened periodically to discuss specific articulation problems and would serve as planning groups for future articulation conferences and workshops. This would permit a more meaningful conference since it would respond to the needs of the regional colleges and be in direct proportion to the institutions in that region. The Bureau of Planning, Department of Education, has established ten regions for higher education planning purposes and articulation. Institutions located in those regions would be served by regional committees.

Although statewide articulation policies and procedures do not exist, Pennsylvania educators suggest in correspondence and conversation that consideration should be given to the following ideas when statewide guidelines are considered: Two-year colleges should discourage students who plan to transfer from concentrating on a major program to the exclusion of general requirements during the first two years. Community college leaders should be interested primarily in establishing policies that assure equal treatment of transfer and enrolled students. Since the four-year college awards the baccalaureate degree in the student's major, it must be in a position to require most of the specialized major work at the senior institution. Four-year colleges should be flexible in accepting course offerings of two-year colleges for elective credit; that is, they should accept a course similar to one offered in the four-year college in the third year for elective credit. This would help to relieve the feeling of the two-year student that he is permitted to take only survey courses for transfer and would give him the opportunity to take a course of special interest during his first two years.

The state university has few articulation problems for students attending one of the commonwealth campuses, as students may complete two years of baccalaureate studies at any of the eighteen locations and automatically transfer to the University Park campus. Associate degree students from the commonwealth campuses may apply for acceptance to baccalaureate programs at University Park under certain conditions and with course credit as evaluated by the dean of the respective colleges. Automatic transfer from community colleges is not assured. Community college graduates are accepted at University Park in competition with other outside transfer students. A course-by-course evaluation of credits is given at the time of admission approval.

The Capitol campus of the State University was founded in 1966. Since its primary responsibility is to award the bachelor of technology degree, community college students transferring to that campus are ordinarily career-program majors in engineering and business-related fields. Since admission is based on a readiness to pursue upper-division work, course-by-course evaluation is not practiced nor are standardized test scores and high school records used for admission.

Minimum requirements are often not sufficient for admission, since admission to upper-division campuses is highly competitive. The minimum cumulative average required for admission to upper-division standing varies from 2.5 to 3.0. For students transferring from an associate degree program in technology, a minimum average of 2.40 is usually required.

Annual visits by the admissions staff to all community colleges, junior colleges, and commonwealth campuses of the university help tremendously in a critical evaluation of each applicant's records. Open lines of communication between two-year college campuses, faculty and staff, and members of the Capitol campus college community help articulation of students to this campus. Students admitted to the Capitol campus generally do not experience a significant change in academic performance from their community college patterns.

Bucknell University, to illustrate the transfer policies of one private institution, does not admit transfer students to a guaranteed junior status. The university evaluates work based on its own course system, credits, and requirements. College performance is more heavily weighed than success in high school or SAT scores. A 2.5 minimum grade point average is required and D grades are not transferred. Although an associate degree is not required for transfer, preference is given to those who have been carrying full academic schedules and have completed many of the general university requirements.

One of the most sensitive areas in articulation is the variation of grade point requirement by senior colleges and universities. Some require a 2.5 average of community college graduates, yet advance their own sophomores with a lower average. Another difficult area, by no means limited to Pennsylvania, is the occasional close scrutiny of community college transcripts by certain university departments. As in many other states, associate degrees in technology continue to be unacceptable.

Discussions and negotiations continue among individual institutions. The Commissioner of Higher Education meets regularly with the heads of the five segments.

Pennsylvania Association for Higher Education. "Articulation Between Two-Year and Four-Year Colleges," November 1969.

Washington Institutional System. Under a 1967 law, the state was divided into twenty-two independent districts with a State Board for Community College Education for coordinating and governing community colleges.

In recent years, attitudes toward two- and four-year college articulation have changed sharply in the state from intense scrutiny of courses by senior institutions to more general acceptance. All public and private senior institutions accept credits from community colleges in a similar manner although requirements vary. Both the University of Washington and the State University have pioneered in establishing good relationships and effective procedures for developing transfer of credit policies; each four-year institution has field representatives who have collectively contributed to the climate of easy transfer.

Western Washington and Central Washington State Colleges generally use the associate in arts degree in meeting general requirements. In 1964 Western Washington State chose a Coordinator of College Relations to be responsible for successful transfer of community college students through the system. The concept continues to gain momentum through the state.

The director of admissions of Washington State University coordinates relations with community colleges. An on-campus conference program, which includes community college and university faculty, is held several times a year. The admissions office also regularly issues a booklet of course equivalencies, *Transfer Programs for Washington Community Colleges.*

A volume published annually by the University of Washington Office of College Relations, *Mobility of Undergraduate College Students Between Washington Colleges and Universities,* reports data for each fall quarter. Another booklet, similar to the Washington State University publication, lists community college transfer and equivalent courses as well as departmental and major requirements. Seattle University produces a similar booklet.

Washington has an unusually good climate for communication in articulation matters. The publications mentioned above have all encouraged formation of both statewide and interinstitutional policy groups, and have contributed significantly to the changing attitude toward articulation. All the state senior institutions have added elements of flexibility to their transfer policies and the same holds true for most of the four-year private institutions.

During fall quarter 1970, the Council on Higher Education directed the various colleges and universities of the state to convene and establish recommendations for the acceptance of the associate in arts degree as common transfer currency. The Washington Council on High School-College Relations reactivated the Inter-College Commission, a subdivision of the parent organization. The commission prepared recommendations for administrators and academic groups within each institution. A tentative plan was developed by the Inter-College Commission and is now under study by each institution.

The prevailing philosophy is that voluntary and cooperative articulation guidelines, based on mutual respect, are significantly more effective than mandatory statewide policies enforced by a centralized state authority.

Specifically the Inter-College Commission pointed out that within the state, opportunities for higher education exist in public and private institutions and these institutions jointly share a responsibility for insuring an orderly progression of students toward completion of degree requirements at all levels. Community college students need assurance that they will have an opportunity to transfer at an appropriate level of advanced standing. Most senior institutions have general education requirements that can be fulfilled in the first two years and community colleges offer similar academic courses. The community colleges offer associate degrees that require completion of general education courses. Several of these degree programs are now accepted in satisfaction of the general education requirements of four-year institutions. It seems desirable and reasonable that associate degrees offered by Washington community colleges should be accepted in satisfaction of the general education requirements of any four-year institution in Washington. The transfer student who has earned an associate degree covered by such agreements should be assured of equal consideration with all other students to continue in junior standing. It is not intended that such an agreement should cause modification of the special requirements (religion, pharmacy, or engineering) of any four-year institution.

These guidelines, implemented by periodic review, provide mutual guarantees of institutional integrity and are consistent with the high level of voluntary cooperation that has become traditional in Washington higher education. Interinstitutional agreements, as recommended by the Inter-College Commission, should generally provide for the fulfillment of college or university general education requirements. It is anticipated that individual institutions may impose certain additional requirements such as religion, philosophy, and so on. The agreements should provide the transferring student with at least ninety quarter credits (or sixty semester credits) upon entry to the four-year institution and provide the transfer student with junior-level standing at entrance.

The associate of arts degree (sometimes called the associate of arts and science degree) is defined in the commission report as that two-year degree offered by the community college to students who have completed the transfer curricula. So that it may be used to fulfill general education requirements for a baccalaureate degree, the associate of arts degree should possess specific characteristics. It should include ninety quarter hours of transferable credit and be issued only to students who have earned a cumulative grade point average of at least 2.0. The degree should allow for completion of approximately two-thirds of the required credits (sixty quarter credits) in general education (also called general university requirements, distribution requirements, breadth requirements) with a reasonable distribution among communication skills, humanities, social sciences, and natural sciences. The associate of arts degree should permit completion of approximately one-half of the unprescribed elective credits in any college courses that the community college will approve for credit toward the associate of arts degree.

An associate of arts agreement applies to general education. Students who transfer within this agreement must still meet lower-division requirements in the major, minor, and professional programs.

Institutions developing mutual agreements must clearly identify degree titles, effective dates, and other specifics to provide clarity for students and advisers and to aid in transcript evaluation. The commission report charts general arts and sciences degree requirements of all public and most private senior colleges and universities. A maximum of one-half the credits required to earn a baccalaureate degree are transferable from two-year colleges. This figure ranges from ninety to ninety-six quarter hours. Each senior institution in the state allows for exceptions if warranted.

The Council on Higher Education has established priorities for admission of transfer students, giving first preference to community college graduates and last to those with less than two years in a two-year college.

Applicants for transfer to the University of Washington must present the high school units specified or the equivalent introductory college courses with five quarter credits treated as the equivalent of one high school unit. Moreover the academic record must show an overall college grade point average of at least 2.00 for residents and 3.00 for out-of-state students. Regardless of the high school record, preference will be given to those who have completed no less than the number of credits specified by the college to which the student is applying. At Washington State University, transfers with less than fifty semester credits (75 quarter) must present a 2.3 grade point average while those with over fifty are admitted on a 2.00.

As indicated earlier, Western and Central Washington State Colleges use the associate in arts degree in meeting general education requirements. The plan developed at Western is outlined for the consideration of other senior institutions interested in examining package transfer agreements.

Associate degrees (full ninety units by mutual agreement) may be used to meet lower-division general education requirements (fifty-four units of fifty-eight general education requirements at Western are lower division). Such contract agreements are currently authorized with nine community colleges. Transfer students are accepted in junior standing without course and credit scrutiny. All collegiate courses that even vaguely relate to a traditional liberal arts curriculum are acceptable (numbered 100 or above). Western is now considering the acceptance of courses in some technical fields, including computer science. Similar agreements exist between eight or nine community colleges and Seattle University and Central Washington State College.

The Seattle University associate of arts degree policies are based on a slightly different concept. The degree itself is not used automatically to meet the lower-division general education requirements. Students who hold the associate of arts degree can transfer all their credits. Seattle University also issues a transfer-guidelines listing similar to those produced by the public universities.

While the Inter-College Commission guidelines allow for interinstitutional agreements on acceptance of occupational courses, they are slow to develop. The University of Washington, however, will now allow a maximum of fifteen quarter credits from occupational studies, either in one area or in composite. Those related to the student's basic objective are usually approved. Some doubt still exists among senior college and university faculty that community colleges offer quality instruction and overcrowded departments make it difficult to observe transfer policies.

Washington State University however has taken the boldest step in announcing full recognition and total acceptance of the associate degree. Students who complete the degree at community colleges in Washington and transfer beginning fall 1972 will be automatically granted full junior standing on completion of all general university graduation requirements.

The universities and other senior institutions, public and private, are moving closer to an unquestioned acceptance of the associate degree as described by the Inter-College Relations Commission. Each senior institution that accepts the transfer guidelines must establish guidelines with other accepting colleges. The case for continuing in that direction is based partly on the fact that it is the usual procedure for transfer at the same level from other senior colleges and universities. The community colleges would determine the student's preparedness for upper-division work, thus eliminating individual course-equivalency evaluation. Washington correspondents agree that the acceptance of the associate degree would greatly expedite transfer procedures that now require extensive personnel.

As in many other states, Washington is moving rapidly toward more centralized authority. It is hoped that the activities of the Inter-College Relations Commission and the Council on Higher Education, emphasizing cooperative and voluntary agreements, will at least supplement if not substitute for this trend.

Inter-College Relations Commission of the Washington Council on High School-College Relations. "Recommended Guidelines for the Development of Inter-Institutional Agreements in Which the Associate of Arts Degree Offered by Community Colleges May be Utilized in Satisfying General Education Requirements of Four-Year Colleges in the State of Washington," March 1971.
Washington State Board for Community College Education. "Survey of High School Relations Activities." Olympia, Washington, October 1971.

6

Voluntary Agreements Among Institutions

Voluntary cooperation and negotiation rather than unilateral declaration or legislative statute is the primary feature of this style. This model relies heavily on regular and individual subject-matter liaison committees created on a temporary or permanent basis to pinpoint problems and to recommend policies and procedures. Decision by agreement rather than edict is, to its advocates, the chief strength. How to put teeth into recommendations from liaison committees is one of the problems. Financing the volunteer organization is a perennial problem in California and Michigan, where this style prevails.

California Articulation Conference Plan

Policies and procedures governing articulation between the University of California (and more recently the California system of state universities and colleges) and the ninety-six California community colleges have developed over a period of several decades largely by voluntary cooperation and negotiation rather than by unilateral declaration or legislation.

The Articulation Conference—an informal body composed of representatives of the four segments of California public education and the private (independent) colleges and universities—has figured prominently in developing this articulation system. The Coordinating Council for Higher Education has exerted pressure on the institutions in favor of mutually acceptable policies on transferability and acceptability of general education courses and graduation requirements.

This system is directly related to statements of function assigned to segments of higher education by *The Master Plan for Higher Education,* portions of which formed the Donahoe Act, 1960. The State of California *Education Code,* on recommendation of the master plan, refers to the university as "primarily academic" (Section 22550). Although the code does not exclude vocational education from university instruction, it does assign such instruction to the junior colleges. Section 7802 states that the junior colleges should prepare persons for agricultural, commercial, homemaking, industrial, and other vocations. The education code also limits the public community colleges to instruction in the thirteenth and fourteenth grades only.

The California articulation plan also reflects mutual agreement on the basic principle that students should be able to move easily and smoothly from the community college to the University of California or state universities and colleges with normal progress. The system is an attempt to make operative the concept shared by university and community college faculties alike that establishing curricula and setting standards for the baccalaureate degree are responsibilities of the faculty.

On July 15, 1969, the Coordinating Council for Higher Education endorsed in principle a joint statement of policy in respect to the admission of eligible applicants for transfer from California public community colleges:

It is mutually agreed by the California community colleges, the California state universities and colleges, and the

University of California that all students who enter California public higher education as freshmen and maintain a satisfactory level of academic performance should be able to progress to the baccalaureate degree without encountering arbitrary barriers to their progress. To this end, the University of California and the California state universities and colleges will give the highest admission priority to transfers from California community public colleges who have completed two years of academic work acceptable for the baccalaureate degree.

If capital or operating funds or faculty are not available, enrollment limitation may become necessary. To assure proper priority, segmental quotas will be established beyond those resulting from campus or college enrollment ceilings or from program control. These quotas will reduce the number admitted from such other categories as first-time freshmen, transfers from institutions other than public community colleges, nonresidents, and graduates.

Qualified community college transfer students who have completed two full years of academic work will receive priority for admission to each segment. Priority of admission to each institution will be consistent with its academic plans; redirection of some eligible community college transfers there may be necessary. Redirection will be accomplished with the minimum possible personal hardship.

University of California Policies and Procedures. The University accepts community college courses equivalent or similar to those offered to university lower-division students. It also accepts community college courses with purpose, scope, and depth appropriate to a university degree, as long as they fit the legally established objectives of the university.

The University Academic Senate, through its Board of Admissions and Relations with Schools, has delegated to the director of admissions and university registrar the authority to determine what courses of an applicant's previous college work may be accepted for advanced standing credit toward a university degree. The director has in turn delegated some of his power to the admissions officers on the several campuses. Any investigation of the status of a community college course therefore begins in the admissions office.

Community college inquiries are normally addressed to the Office of Relations with Schools on the nearest university campus and are forwarded to the Universitywide Office of Admissions. If new courses are involved, the inquiry is expected to include a brief description of material covered. Copies of such inquiries are also sent to the associate director (Office of Relations with Schools) in charge of University-Community College articulation on the Los Angeles campus.

If the community college course is found transferable, it is automatically applied toward a degree from any campus of the university. On some campuses the admissions officer will designate the community college course as equivalent to a course given on that campus (that is, Economics forty-one at a community college is equivalent to UCLA Economics five); on others such as Berkeley it will be noted simply as three units of economics credit. Courses that have no counterpart on the campus will be accepted for credit by title.

The dean determines such advanced-standing credit toward graduation requirements from a particular college or school of the university. He is the administrative representative of the faculty that established the requirements and is expected to be discriminating in his decisions. The dean is not bound by the statement of equivalency provided by the office of admissions, but in practice he is usually guided by its findings. He will also determine (sometimes after consultation with the appropriate departmental chairmen) whether or not a community college course meets a departmental prerequisite for an academic major. Only the dean can determine if a particular course will satisfy a breadth requirement or a requirement for an academic major. Even when the dean's decision is negative, the student retains elective credit toward graduation.

A system of internal bookkeeping on course clearance is maintained, including a code identification assigned to each request by the initiating relations with schools officer. These universitywide officers work directly with articulation specialists chosen by each community college as liaison officers.

State Universities and Colleges Policies and Procedures. Articulation policies of the California state college system have in recent years undergone sweeping changes. Beginning in 1969 (according to amendments to Title Five of the *California Education Code*), up to forty units of general education from a California community college would be accepted at full face value. Under that policy, any state college was allowed to determine general education requirements beyond the fifty-unit maximum if these applied equally to both the transfer and the nontransfer student. Some community colleges wished to encourage career courses such as agriculture and business education.

Amendments to the Title Five sections, which include the state college undergraduate admission policy, would make credit for admission purposes and degree purposes the same. Sixty transferable units from community colleges must be accepted by the particular state college or state university. September 1, 1974, was set as the effective date.

As a counterproposal, the Board of Governors of the California Community Colleges requested that state universities and colleges accept community college presidents' certification of acceptable college credit units within the guidelines to be established. The definition of units acceptable for admission of "any course equivalent or acceptable to any state university or college will be acceptable to all" was requested as the basic guideline principle. At this time all units taken in community colleges are used to determine eligibility for admission to a state college. The proposed change for undergraduate transfer admission to the state universities and colleges would allow students to use only those units transferable for baccalaureate degree purposes in determining eligibility for admission.

All segments of public higher education in California—the university, the state universities and colleges, and the community colleges—share responsibility for difficulties that tend to block the smooth operation of the California plan of articulation. Differences in philosophy exist. The university maintains exacting entrance requirements and insists on rigorous academic performance. Community colleges, as open door institutions, take students where they find them and permit more flexible standards. There are signs however that the university is becoming more flexible and the community colleges more exacting. Beginning with the 1973–1974 academic year, mandated specific courses for the community college associate in arts degree will be replaced by several general but sweeping requirements. Specifically, fifteen semester units will be required for the degree in four fields: natural sciences (such as biology, chemistry, and physics); humanities, such as languages, literature, and philosophy; learning skills, such as oral and written communication; and logic, mathematics, and statistics, which are intended to facilitate knowledge in natural sciences, social sciences, and humanities. At least one course would be required in each of the four fields and ethnic studies must be offered in one or more of the four fields.

The University of California now accepts up to sixteen quarter units of work transferred from community colleges to replace courses in which D or F grades were earned. Repeated courses must be exact repetitions. Colleges of letters and science on several university campuses, notably UCLA and UC Berkeley, have abandoned foreign language graduation requirements.

Studies recently prepared for the Coordinating Council for Higher Education have uncovered no major obstacles facing the community college student who plans to transfer to the University of California. Transferability of courses is to be determined by procedures now in effect. Community college courses to be used in fulfilling breadth requirements are to be named by the community college concerned, subject to review and acceptance by the faculty of the university or state college concerned.

The university will continue its efforts to encourage greater mutual acceptability of breadth requirements among the colleges of letters and science and their equivalents on all campuses and greater flexibility in accepting work completed in community college toward fulfillment of breadth requirements.

As described earlier, state college–community college articulation policies are being negotiated. Joint committees are working on definition of terms such as *transferable* and *acceptable,* and other detailed provisions of the agreement.

California Community Colleges 1972 Directory. Sacramento: Office of the Chancellor, California Community Colleges.

Coordinating Council for Higher Education. *Resolution 322.* July 15, 1969.

University of California. *Articulation, University of California and
California Public Junior Colleges.* Berkeley: Office of the
President, 1968.

Michigan Modified Articulation Conference Plan

The State Board of Public and Community Colleges advises
the State Board of Education on the supervision of the twenty-nine
public two-year colleges in Michigan. State legislation in 1965 gave
organizing and bargaining right to public employees, including
community college faculties. The state board has recently begun
to exert control over community college curriculum planning. All
curricula must be approved by that body. Up to the present, articulation between two- and four-year colleges has been developed by
the Michigan Association of Collegiate Registrars and Admissions
Officers in a cooperative and voluntary relationship.

For many years, the University of Michigan has maintained
a Bureau of School Services responsible for accreditation of secondary schools and for liaison with community colleges. The university
has an assistant director of admissions for community college services, as do most of the other public senior institutions. Michigan
State University, Western Michigan University, and Eastern Michigan University accept more community college transfer students
than does the University of Michigan.

A transfer orientation program has been developed at
Michigan State University. Before registration, transfer students
meet with a representative of the university college, who explains
basic requirements and credit evaluation and arranges academic
advising. The office of orientation provides a variety of services
to enable students to begin classes with a minimum of difficulty.

A philosophy of cooperation and flexibility is practiced
among community colleges and senior institutions in Michigan.
Room to maneuver is allowed for handling unusual and individual
transfer situations. Authority to determine course transferability
rests with the receiving institution. A course syllabus may be requested and in a small number of cases may be referred to the
appropriate university department for the transfer decision. All
decisions are relayed annually to concerned institutions. *Report of*

Acceptance and Application of Community College Credits Toward Degree Requirements at Four-Year Institutions gives concise transfer information about most senior colleges and universities in Michigan.

At the University of Michigan, decisions on specific degree requirements are made by a board or committee of each school or college, which then follows its own guidelines. Faculty is also consulted on such cases as seminars, independent study, and field courses.

Through the years the Michigan Association of Collegiate Registrars and Admissions Officers has promoted uniformity in transfer policies. Unlike the University of Michigan, several senior institutions accept selected vocational-technical courses.

Private universities supply community colleges with course equivalency guides as far as possible. However unlike the state-supported schools, private institutions are not allowed to have degree requirements and recommended course outlines printed in community college catalogues. This restriction on private schools is the result of a regulation by the Michigan Board of Education.

An important document developed and unanimously approved by a joint committee sponsored by the Michigan Association of Collegiate Registrars and Admission Officers is being widely discussed. The proposal for *A Statewide Articulation Agreement Regarding Basic Two-year Requirements* provides a middle ground that hopefully will be acceptable to the faculties of the public and private senior institutions. The proposal, described below, combats the lack of continuity in two- and four-year academic programs. The intent of this proposal is to insure that a student who completes an associate degree at a Michigan public community college will have satisfied the basic two-year requirements of all public four-year institutions in the state.

The proposal should require the agreement of both the two- and four-year institutions on the nature, content, and extent of minimum basic two-year requirements. The following statements are proposed as integral parts of such an agreement:

Basic requirements are defined as those requirements designed to provide students with a broad intellectual experience in the major fields of knowledge. The intent of such requirements is to ensure that each graduate will have experienced some of the content, method, and system of values of the various disciplines that enable man to understand himself and his environment.

Basic two-year requirements will include English composition and the broad categories of social science, natural science, and humanities. The inclusion of specific courses within a given category would be determined by the faculty offering the course. For example, a western civilization course might be appropriately designated as either social science or humanities, depending on the content. Mathematics would be included in the natural science category. Nontransferable technical, vocational, or developmental courses will not be included in the basic requirements. As foreign language is not required for any junior college degree programs, no foreign language stipulations will be included in this agreement. Foreign language requirements for individual baccalaureate degree programs will be the prerogative of the senior institutions.

Each receiving institution will determine the equivalence and applicability of basic two-year courses in meeting other graduation requirements. The receiving institution may not however require additional basic two-year requirements, regardless of the individual course evaluations, if the transfer student has received the A.A. or A.S. degree. A student who has completed the basic two-year requirements, but not the associate degree, will not be required to pursue further basic courses in the receiving institution. Transfer students who have not completed the basic two-year requirements of the community college will meet the requirements of the four-year institution as determined by an individual evaluation of his previous work.

The adoption of a statewide code establishing basic principles and curriculum for transfer students would seem highly desirable from several viewpoints. Under such a code, students in the community colleges would be able to explore several areas without having to commit themselves to a particular academic program and institution at the time of their first enrollment. At the present time, community college students may lose time and credit if they are not ready to make career decisions when they enter a community college; most four-year institutions allow their native students two years of exploration time. In addition, students would be able to meet the necessary transfer requirements without the necessity of getting into a course offered only once a year or one that might be dropped because of low enrollment.

The code would also benefit faculty, who could provide a curriculum that would better meet the needs of their students without having to provide specific courses as requirements of the various four-year institutions. Faculty could also do a better job of counseling students if the four-year institutional requirements were more nearly uniform.

Counseling services would be greatly improved under a uniform code simply because counselors could spend more time counseling students without having to absorb the enormous and varied data on general degree requirements of the four-year institutions. It would also result in much more efficient counseling in community colleges that have a high counselor turnover.

The adoption of a general curricular articulation agreement in Michigan would not affect the autonomy of individual institutions to introduce new courses or programs, to establish concentrated prerequisites to determine specific requirements for native students, to evaluate the transferability of individual courses, or to require certain levels of quality for entrance. It would however insure that a student with an associate degree from a Michigan community college would not be required to pursue further general education requirements at any four-year college or university. This would greatly improve the articulation of colleges and universities in Michigan and would provide a degree of uniformity badly needed by students, faculty, counselors, and administrators.

Agreements of this nature are not new in higher education. California, for example, has a statewide statutory code regulating the curricular articulation of two- and four-year institutions. This code specifies in general terms the minimum number of credit hours necessary in general education areas. It would seem likely that without this kind of regulation, the large and complex higher education system of California would have chaotic articulation problems.

Although voluntary articulation has proved successful in Michigan, there is increasing evidence that the future will bring greater control by state agencies. At the present time, a bill has been proposed amending the state constitution to limit the constitutional autonomy of state colleges and universities.

Articulation Committee of the Michigan Association of Collegiate Registrars and Admissions Officers. *Proposal for a Statewide Articulation Agreement Regarding Basic Two-Year Requirements.* 1971.

 7

Developments in
Other States

Only twenty-two states have developed articulation programs that fit one of the models in Chapters Four, Five, and Six. The vast majority, however, have taken initial steps toward instituting transfer systems. Invariably, the first step is the creation of joint committees to develop guideline statements acceptable to both the two- and the four-year institutions. This chapter concentrates on developments in the remaining twenty-eight states and the District of Columbia, where articulation plans or combinations of plans are yet to be clarified. Articulation in these states is frequently handled on an individual student basis.

Alabama

The Alabama Commission on Higher Education, as the coordinating agency for all higher education, has overall responsibility for junior-senior college articulation. This function is still performed largely on the institutional level within the boundaries of statewide policy decisions. Academic programs throughout the state system are based on university and senior college curricula. Transfer from the eighteen junior colleges to senior colleges and universities operates smoothly, largely because of the mutually agreed role definitions. The legislative act that created the state junior college system did not include a section on course credit acceptance. Through the years however the universities and state colleges have developed a framework of transfer procedures with junior colleges. A joint junior-senior college articulation committee may be created to detail transfer guidelines. This committee would be similar to the Florida TASK Force.

Alaska

The eight public community colleges in Alaska belong to the University of Alaska system. The University Vice-President for Public Service provides statewide coordination and liaison of community colleges. Vocational-technical training is provided by community colleges under contract with the local school board. The university is essentially responsible for academic programs. Transfer courses are therefore evaluated by the university registrar and approved by the department head after students are admitted. Transfer students with less than thirty acceptable credits are required to take American College Testing Service tests before their applications are processed.

Arkansas

The Arkansas general assembly passed legislation in 1965 to permit municipalities, counties, or groups of counties to create community college districts. A Commission on Coordination of Higher Educational Finance (the State Community Junior College Board) coordinates establishment of a comprehensive two-year college, which is considered a local institution. Each Arkansas community junior college is governed by a separate local board. The commission recently released an influential booklet, *The Community Junior College Story,* which sets forth three plans for identifying potential community college areas, following the basic philosophy that all counties would eventually be served by comprehensive colleges. A master plan is now being developed.

No formal articulation agreements exist between junior and senior institutions. The Commission on Coordination of Higher Educational Finance encourages ease of transfer from junior to senior institutions. Many students transfer to the university before receiving the associate degree, some with only a few semesters of work. All credit, including some in vocational classes earned at an accredited community college, is accepted by the University of Arkansas; for example, the university will transfer ninety units of agriculture toward graduation.

Commission on Coordination of Higher Educational Finance. *The Community Junior College Story.* Little Rock, Arkansas: State Community Junior College Board, November 1969.

Colorado

The community college system was created by the 1967 legislature under the jurisdiction of the State Board for Community Colleges and Occupational Education. New colleges were established under the legislation and existing local district colleges were given the option of becoming part of the state system or remaining as local district institutions. The legislature charged the State Board for Community Colleges and Occupational Education, in cooperation with the Colorado Commission on Higher Education, to assume the responsibility for recommending and reviewing all curricula, defining degrees, approving administration and budgets, and setting state community college policy. Statewide articulation policies are being developed by the State Board for Community Colleges and Occupational Education staff and are being coordinated through the College Council on High School–College Relations. Currently each institution has its own separate policy on articulation. Transfer credits are broadly accepted from the two-year colleges to the four-year colleges, but special problems arise in course equivalence because of the lack of communication and coordination.

Articulation problems will be eased with the development of statewide guidelines and standard course equivalencies for lower-division programs. The commission on higher education is presently working with the State Board for Community Colleges and Occupational Education on these two projects. A subcommittee of the Colorado Association of Community and Junior Colleges is attempting to strengthen community college–high school articulation, and the Instructional Deans' Association is preparing a position paper on two-year four-year college articulation.

A counselor handbook is published annually by the Colorado Council on High School–College Relations and provides a wide variety of information on institutions of higher education.

Connecticut

A state system of higher education was established in 1965, including a State Board of Trustees for Regional Community Colleges. The Commission for Higher Education is the coordinating body for the University of Connecticut state colleges, regional community colleges, and state technical colleges. Each segment has its own board of trustees. The commission has recently published *Guidebook on Transfer,* which contains information from public and private senior colleges and universities on admissions, requirements, special programs, and so on. Task forces on higher education planned by the commission have submitted priority recommendations to the governor and the state general assembly. Community colleges, through the state officer, have working transfer agreements with four state colleges whereby qualified graduates may enter as juniors. The state university offers similar opportunities for transfer of community college students. A comprehensive articulation study is presently under way involving both public and private colleges.

Delaware

The Delaware Technical and Community College, with northern and southern branches, is supported and operated by the state. The institution grants associate in applied science degrees, primarily in business and engineering technologies. Both campuses require general education in their technical education majors. Institutional leaders of the state meet regularly over articulation matters. Residents of Delaware may pursue the associate in science or arts in the liberal arts program contracted to the University of

Delaware. The general studies area is a certificate course of study designed to prepare students for degree-granting programs. It is essentially programmed, almost tutorial in nature. The office of the Assistant Dean for College Parallel Program is responsible for the coordination between the university and the public community college. The staff is made up of university employees.

A philosophy of reciprocal admission is maintained between the Technical and Community College and the University of Delaware. Liberal arts students at the Technical and Community College have dual academic status in that they are considered both university as well as technical and community college students. Since the University of Delaware handles admission and instruction, these students may transfer automatically to the Newark campus of the university. Transfer students are encouraged to complete at least one full academic year of college before applying to the university.

At the Delaware Technical and Community College, a performance evaluation has replaced the traditional letter grade system. This is based on a philosophy of success rather than a concern with failure, and students are evaluated in terms of measurable behavioral objectives established for every course. Satisfactory performance is recognized as *proficient*. The term *distinctive* is used for excellent performance. The term *recycle* refers to less than satisfactory performance. Students receiving a recycle evaluation can strengthen the weak performance areas to earn a proficient evaluation. A technical profile is developed on each graduate and indicates strengths and weaknesses to potential employers and to transfer institutions as well. The system also includes the traditional grades—w-official, w-unofficial, and incomplete—but the technical profile is the viable record.

To sum up, the college is primarily interested in what students know when they leave.

District of Columbia

While the District of Columbia does not have a system of higher education, it has five good-sized universities, several smaller colleges, a two-year college (primarily transfer), and a technical institute. One of the three institutions offering associate degrees, Northeastern University, a college of business and financial administration, also confers the baccalaureate. Originally organized as a YMCA College, Northeastern University was awarded a federal charter in 1937 by the Seventy-Fifth Congress, placing administrative and financial direction under its board of trustees.

There is no formal program of articulation for junior-senior college transfer. Transcripts are examined individually by colleges and local acceptability determination is made by the senior institution. The usual criteria of accreditation, grade point average, and grades are bases for transfer.

George Washington University admits probably more transfers than any other institution in the city. In the fall of 1971, 600 of the 1000 students were transfers. Federal City College, established in 1970, is also primarily a transfer institution.

Idaho

The state board of education is the coordinating agency for the two community colleges; each institution however is operated by an elected local board of trustees. Despite the fact that Boise College, long an influential two-year college, became a state four-year college, general support of junior college education has not diminished. Ricks College, a private church-related junior college founded in 1915, is currently the largest in the state. By state statute, junior college credits earned up to a maximum of one-half the total required for the baccalaureate degree will be transferred.

Indiana

This state does not have a system of public community colleges. It has one public junior college—Vincennes University, which since the 1870s has been described as a junior college—and two private junior colleges accredited for teacher education. Some private two-year institutions are oriented toward vocational-technical education and others toward specializations in religion, fine arts, and other fields. The four major state universities operate branch campuses in all the well-populated centers of the state. Both career-oriented and degree programs are offered. The availability of such programs on nearly twenty campuses has decreased the demand for legislation to authorize community junior colleges. Indiana University and various two-year colleges have a long history of cooperation in maintaining similarity of courses and transfer of credit. The five public universities supply a large portion of the technical education offered in the state.

Kansas

The Community Junior College Act of 1965 established a state system of two-year colleges with the State Superintendent of Public Instruction as the state authority and an Advisory Council for Community Junior Colleges. The State Commissioner of Education is currently the state authority. Most of the colleges are countywide districts. About one-fourth of the students are enrolled in vocational programs.

A statewide committee, known as the Master Planning Commission, was established by the 1970 Kansas legislature to prepare the first phase of a master plan on education. Under the direction of Professor Kenneth E. Anderson (University of Kansas), the committee has produced three publications: *Enrollment Projections, Educational Planning to 1985,* and *Educational and Training Requirements of the Kansas Economy to 1985.* In a four-volume report, the commission presented a comprehensive inventory of student needs and aspirations resulting from eleven surveys and comparisons. Few states can match the magnitude of the Kansas educational-needs inventory.

Transfer students from community junior colleges are admitted to the University of Kansas on a selective basic. A resolution is currently before the University Board of Regents that graduates of community junior colleges be considered to have completed university general education requirements. A c average is the minimum transfer grade point average. Except in meritorious cases, no advanced-standing credit is awarded to a student for work done in a two-year college after he has completed the equivalent of the first two years of work in any curriculum. In such cases, credit is not to exceed eight semester hours and must be approved by the student's dean in advance. Courses must be substantially equivalent to courses offered by the University of Kansas. If courses are not exactly equivalent but are transferable, they are identified as accurately as possible and used to fulfill graduation requirements. How these or any other courses are used toward degree requirements is determined by the dean of each specific school. Vocational-technical courses may transfer if these are of collegiate quality and the receiving institution offers a degree in the special field.

Articulation is to be investigated by the master planning commission.

Kansas Master Plan Commission. *Educational Planning to 1985: Interim Report.* Topeka, Kansas. Master Plan Commission, December 1970a.
Kansas Master Plan Commission. *Projection: Grade Twelve Enrollments in Kansas Public and Private High Schools 1970–71 to 1986–87,* December 1970b.
Kansas Master Plan Commission. *Student Needs, Aspirations, and Accomplishments: Essential Ingredients in State Planning for Post Secondary Education,* March 1972.

Louisiana

The state has two public community colleges. Three branches of Louisiana State University offer academic as well as occupational programs. Two pilot two-year programs are connected with high schools. The university will not accept more than one-half the credit required for a degree from two-year colleges. All transfer students with fewer than thirty semester hours are enrolled in the junior division of the university. A junior-division council serves as liaison between the division and other university units. A master plan is being developed by the Coordinating Council for Higher Education.

Maine

Maine does not have a public community college. Two of the eight branches of the University of Maine offer two-year career courses and university-parallel programs. A feasibility study of a community college system was discussed in a 1966 study of higher education, but no action has been taken. Admission of transfer students to the university is on a selective basis.

Maryland

The tripartite system of higher education, which includes sixteen community colleges, is coordinated by the Council for Higher Education. The State Board for Community Colleges has been in operation since 1969, with the responsibility for facilitating transfer of students between community colleges and other public senior institutions. A study advisory committee on Patterns of Academic Success (PAS) has been appointed to study articulation issues and to eliminate problems. It is expected that the completion of the articulation and PAS studies will improve intersegmental cooperation and result in smoother articulation. The State Board for Community Colleges staff intends to give particular attention to the articulation of returning veterans, disadvantaged youth, and secondary school graduates. The staff will also continue to collect articulation information from other states and measure the appropriateness of other transfer processes in the higher education system of Maryland.

Minnesota

Twenty public two-year colleges all belong to the statewide system. The State Junior College Board appointed by the governor is the single policy-making board for the system. Individual campuses are served by advisory boards appointed by the state board. In addition to the General College on the main campus, the University of Minnesota operates two satellite two-year technical schools on sites previously used as resident agricultural high schools. Articulation is an individual relationship between institutions. An increasing number of articulation conferences are being held.

Mississippi

The eighteen public junior colleges in Mississippi are controlled by local boards of trustees. The state board of education and the Junior College Commission have supervisory and coordinating responsibilities. A Junior-Senior College Conference is held annually and articulation problems are freely discussed. Junior college transfer credits are accepted by the senior colleges and universities without question. Excellent coordination exists between state agencies, the university, and the junior colleges.

Montana

The executive secretary of the university system has recently been appointed the coordinator of community college districts. The state board of education is the supervisory agency. A master plan for community colleges is now complete. At present, university acceptance of community college credit is based on recommendations found in *Report of Credit Given by Educational Institutions,* issued by the American Association of Collegiate Registrars and Admissions Officers. Equivalent or similar courses are uniformly accepted by the three university branches. Technical course credit may be transferred if authorized by a departmental chairman. Additional credits over the maximum will be accepted upon approval of a dean or chairman.

Nebraska

New legislation provides for establishment of a community college system in Nebraska under the title Technical Community Colleges. A state director will coordinate the new State Board for Technical Community Colleges. The plan will be effective in July 1973, when the existing six public junior colleges and eight state technical colleges will all have been transferred to the new community college districts.

Articulation continues to improve. Although a state plan has not developed, broad approval of transfer programs has been achieved. An advisors' handbook for use in community colleges is prepared annually by the Nebraska Association of Collegiate Registrars and Admissions Officers. The University of Nebraska hosts an annual articulation conference. The four-year colleges vary in acceptance of junior college credit from sixty to sixty-six hours. Hours earned in technical programs in the technical colleges are recognized by the University of Nebraska and by Kearney State

College for application toward degrees in industrial education. Other institutions of the state are moving toward similar practices. Establishment of suitable identification of technical courses that deserve consideration for academic credit is a current problem. The community colleges are listed in the AACRAO *Report of Credit Given By Educational Institutions* with an A rating, indicating that credit is accepted, but the seven technical colleges are not listed. However the technical colleges will be listed in the next report with a B rating (credit accepted on a limited basis). It is anticipated that the technical colleges will be continued on that rating as they come into the new system, and when they have established transfer programs they will be given the A rating.

New Hampshire

The only institution in New Hampshire referred to as a public two-year college is the New Hampshire Technical Institute at Concord. A comparable-course philosophy is used by the university in making transfer decisions. The American Association of Collegiate Registrars and Admissions Officers' document, *Report of Credit Given by Educational Institutions,* is the basic transfer guide.

New Mexico

The public junior college at Hobbs, opened in 1967, is the only two-year institution independent of university control. Two of Eastern New Mexico University's three branches are called community colleges. The AACRAO document is generally used as a transfer guide by all state-supported and private universities. At the University of New Mexico, transfer courses are evaluated by the office of admissions. The college dean determines course equivalency for specific degree programs and prepares statements of remaining degree requirements for transfer students.

North Dakota

Guidelines adopted by the state board of education are used by senior institutions to accept transfer students from the five two-year colleges in North Dakota. Programs for accepted students are developed on an individual basis, often in consultation with the head of the student's major department. Transfer students from junior colleges must have achieved academic standards equivalent to comparable resident students in that institution and must complete a minimum of sixty semester hours or ninety quarter hours of the baccalaureate degree requirements at degree-granting institutions. Transfer credits from two-year colleges will be counted only in those courses offered at the degree-granting institution as freshman and sophomore courses. The above stipulations do not apply to vocational students.

The University of North Dakota at Grand Forks enrolls transfer students with fewer than twenty-four semester hours in the university college. Those transferring with more than twenty-four but fewer than sixty hours may enter the degree college, but still must meet general graduation requirements. Transfer credit is still provisional and subject to revision at the end of the first year. Although the transfer system is working well, all institutions of postsecondary education are currently reviewing the total articulation process. This will include matters of accommodation for students and review of courses eligible for transfer.

North Dakota State Colleges and Universities. *Articulation and Coordination Conference.* October 1971.

Ohio

All twenty branches of the state university offer two-year degrees. All types of two-year institutions—including four comprehensive community colleges, seventeen technical institutions, and the university branches—are coordinated by the Ohio Board of Regents.

While no specific articulation plan has been approved, an advisory committee has recently been appointed by the Board of Regents to deal with transfer of general education courses and introductory professional curricula. Transfer cases are handled by university admissions on an individual basis. Several state universities in Ohio have developed four-year technology programs that accept most of the credits from a two-year technical education program. There is no uniform policy however among the state universities on the acceptance of two-year credits in nontraditional courses. This has been confusing to students and educators alike.

Two documents, in addition to the 1970 master plan statement, support the need for attention to articulation: *Standards for the Approval of Associate Degrees in Two-Year Technologies,* released by the Ohio Board of Regents in 1965, and a resolution adopted in December 1970 by the Board of Higher Education on *Transfer Equivalency of the Junior-Community Associate Degree in Baccalaureate Sequences.* Articulation conferences on particular transfer-fields have been initiated as forerunners of agreements.

Ohio Board of Regents. "Standards for the Approval of Associate Degrees in Two-Year Technologies." Columbus, Ohio, May 1965.

Rhode Island

The Commission to Study Higher Education recommended the establishment of a statewide system of junior colleges with facilities in the Pawtuxet Valley, Blackstone Valley, and the Mount Hope area of Rhode Island. The first of the state system of junior colleges was established in 1964 under the name of Rhode Island Junior College. The University of Rhode Island restricts the number of transfer students from junior colleges to available space. Efforts to improve accommodations have increased junior and senior transfers to about 500 per year. In most instances an incoming junior college freshman can be advised about specific academic requirements at either the college or university and arrange his program of studies accordingly. At the time of graduation a qualified student should find admission at either four-year institution quite likely with a minimum loss of credits (usually from three to nine semester hours).

Because of interinstitutional communication involving deans or department heads of the junior college and their corresponding colleagues in upper-level institutions, most courses offered for transfer credits at Rhode Island Junior College are equivalent to courses given on the four-year level or are given elective credit. Each of the four-year public institutions is undergoing major curriculum revisions. Such changes will necessitate new plans for acceptability of courses by upper-level institutions and also in the program planning of junior college students. There is a clear need for cooperative planning by joint junior college–university curriculum committees to insure greater integration of programming.

South Carolina

Although private junior colleges have served the state since 1927, South Carolina does not have a public community college. College-parallel programs are provided locally by regional campuses or branches of the University of South Carolina and Clemson University. Twelve technical education centers with low tuition cover most of the state, offering skill and technical courses that include programs leading to the associate in applied science degree. Local committees give the offerings a community orientation, although governance is provided by the State Advisory Committee for Technical Education. The State Commission for Higher Education is a coordinating body, and as such deals indirectly with both technical education centers and branch campuses of the universities.

With the exception of some new experimental programs, regulations controlling admissions to the regional campuses of the universities are the same as those for the regular universities. Officials of four-year institutions of higher education have hesitated to accept courses in transfer from technical education centers. However those centers have recently been accredited by the Southern Association of Colleges and Schools, and four-year institutions are in the process of reexamining their policies.

A committee is presently operating under legislative mandate to devise a plan for a system of comprehensive community colleges, which would increase flexibility and reduce duplication. Should this system fail to win legislative support, it is certain that efforts will still be made to increase cooperation between technical education centers and the regional campuses.

South Dakota

One of the alternative proposals of the South Dakota master plan for public higher education presented in December 1970 was to merge Southern State College at Springfield with the University of South Dakota at Vermillion, to develop a technical school in addition to the academic program. The South Dakota Legislature passed a bill that directed this change. The Regents of Education adopted a resolution with the same intent in January 1971. It is not anticipated however that a public community college system will be developed. Transfer requests are handled on an individual basis. Public senior institutions and some private schools limit credits from junior colleges to sixty-four through sixty-eight, two years of work, or half the number of credits required for the baccalaureate degree. The South Dakota Post High School Coordinating Council has been created to help develop articulation agreements.

Tennessee

Public two-year colleges were first authorized in 1965 by the state board of education. A higher education commission has recently been appointed to coordinate the development of more community colleges; eight are now operating. A state master plan is now being prepared. The newly organized Committee on Articulation with Other Schools of the University of Tennessee is primarily concerned with junior college transfer students who have difficulty beginning their upper-division work. Guidelines for improving communication between two-year and four-year institutions have been developed by the University of Tennessee Committee on Articulation. The committee has initiated meetings of department heads, key faculty, and academic administrators of the university and junior colleges to deal with issues involving articulation of curriculum and admission policies.

Utah

The two-year college system is composed of three comprehensive community colleges and two technical colleges. Some senior colleges offer extensive technical programs; this includes Weber State, originally a junior college. Graduates of the junior colleges with associate degrees transfer to the University of Utah with all general education requirements fulfilled. In most university departments, completion of general education requirements is not prerequisite to pursuing a major. Since transfer numbers are small, transfers are handled individually. The two-year college program is not likely to expand.

Institutional Council, Utah State University. *General Education Program: Guidelines for Course Design.* 1972.

Vermont

This state supports a regional college and a public technical college. The Vermont Regional Community College was created by an executive order of the governor in 1970. Partly financed under a three-year U. S. Office of Education grant, this institution serves three regions of the state. The college does not have a central campus; administrative offices are located in Montpellier, the capital city; permanent staff live and work in the regional centers where community buildings are used for classes. About 50 percent of the students are enrolled in vocational classes. The vocational-technical curricula are developed in close coordination with the Vermont Technical Institute.

The university, the state colleges, and private junior colleges are operated by different boards of trustees, and while a few students transfer each year the university is not obliged to accept transfers from state or junior colleges. One of the recommendations before the state legislative body is the proposed merger of the university, the four state colleges, and the two-year colleges under one governing board.

Vermont Regional Community College Commission: Present and Future. (Prepared by the Commission for the Joint Senate-House Committee on Education, Subcommittee on Higher Education) September 1971.

West Virginia

A single board for all higher education—the West Virginia Board of Regents—was created by the legislature in 1969. Action by the 1971 legislature empowered the Board of Regents to convert any one, several, or all of the existing two-year branch colleges of senior colleges and universities into community colleges. This conversion is in process. Development of a state system is predicated on the full transfer of credits and grades from one state institution to another institution. The Board of Regents holds the view that the system should promote flexibility for the students and that college work earned at one institution is equal to that earned at any other institution in the state. Specific policies and procedures for the state system are being developed. The Board of Regents has announced that there will be a full transferability of college-parallel credit from a community college to any of the state four-year colleges or two universities.

Wyoming

The Wyoming Higher Education Council, a seven-member council appointed by the governor, coordinates all higher education in the state. A community college commission was recently created by the legislature with primary responsibility for extending communication among the seven community colleges. Transfer applications are handled on an individual basis. A joint Colorado-Wyoming junior-senior college relations committee of the American Association of Collegiate Registrars and Admissions Officers is active in articulation matters.

Summary

Transfer admissions is now priority business in all but a few states. Statewide plans, beginning initially with guidelines later to be translated into policies, are appearing in state after state. These have occurred first where so many students are involved that senior institutions can no longer continue making transfer decisions on an individual student basis. Statewide guidelines however deal primarily with course and program articulation, and unfortunately are far less concerned with the accommodation of students.

Statewide articulation organization is also accelerated where senior colleges and universities are experiencing lags in enrollments. This recent phenomenon, coupled with the current widespread lack of public confidence in higher education, has resulted in heavy budgetary cutbacks.

For reasons at least partly budgetary, major universities are intensifying efforts to attract transfer students. Senior institutions, public and private alike, are soliciting community college graduates. The University of California system, for example, has recently reduced its entrance grade point average from 2.4 to 2.0 for community college transfers who were not eligible at high school graduation. All campuses in the system have also initiated or increased recruitment activities. For the first time in their long history as a multiversity, the eight general campuses are competing with each other for students, transfers as well as freshmen.

Development of state systems of articulation has also resulted from the landmark work of the AAC-AAJC-AACRAO Joint Committee on Junior and Senior Colleges in the development of the 1966 "Guidelines," and from the comprehensive research conducted by Knoell and Medsker (see Chapter One). Organizations, including certain regional accrediting agencies and to a much greater extent the American Association of Collegiate Registrars and Admissions Officers, continue to exert pressure for better articulation.

Compatibility of certain occupational programs has provided impetus in specific areas where baccalaureate degrees have been developed by senior institutions. While as yet limited, this factor has striking future potential.

"The Articulation Scene," Part 2, identified the trend toward state systems. As illustrated in the three models outlined in this section, articulation in most of the fifty states appears destined to be a statewide effort. At best these plans would be conceived and developed by broad consensus paralleling the general *Guidelines* released in 1966 by the Joint Committee on Junior and Senior Colleges. At worst the statewide policies would appear as legislative mandates to be enforced by a state agency.

The "Model for Developing Solutions to Articulation Problems on a Statewide Basis," developed by Wattenbarger (Figure 1), exemplifies the full and continuous participation essential to the long-term success of a plan. It provides the legal structure for recognizing problems, gathering reactions, and implementing solutions. It further includes the grass roots level in the communication system.

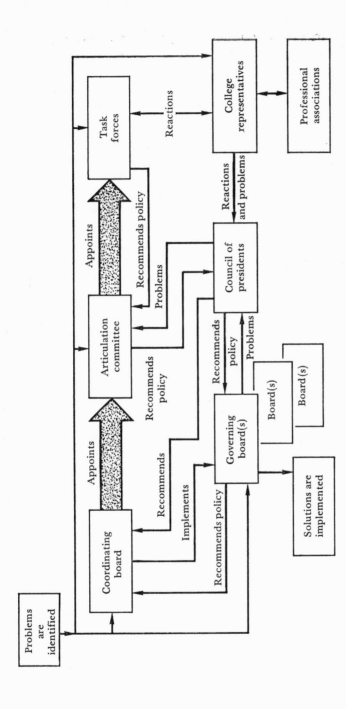

FIGURE 1. Model for developing solutions to articulation problems on a statewide basis (from Wattenbarger, 1972).

To this model should be added an appeal system beginning with an appeal from individual students. Inasmuch as the student is the focus of a transfer complaint, any model, as Wattenbarger indicates, should be for the benefit of the student. Constant efforts must be made to inform students of appeal routes.

The Wattenbarger model includes professional organizations. Most influential of these are the regional accrediting agencies and associations, including representatives of all accredited collegiate institutions and other associations such as the American Association of Collegiate Registrars and Admissions Officers. Although the accrediting agencies have as yet had little to do with articulation beyond high school-to-college transition, the association continues to be a powerful agency in many states on articulation matters. Its *Report of Credit Given,* an annual summary of credit acceptance policies, serves as an articulation guide in a number of states including Montana, Nebraska, Nevada, New Hampshire, New Mexico, and Wyoming. AACRAO is a strong influence in such other states as Colorado and Wisconsin and is still probably the most potent force in the changing Michigan scene.

The model establishes the machinery for a constant flow of communication including the implementation of solutions. It further provides for contributions from various members of the college communities on a volunteer basis.

Articulation was defined in Part One as both a process and an attitude. The point was made that the success of the process depends on the willingness of responsible personnel to place the student ahead of administrative expediency. Since willingness to volunteer generally indicates a desire to serve in the best interest, an articulation model should necessarily provide for a voluntary peer-level contribution.

8

The Canadian Scene

The Canadian scene of postsecondary education, particularly in patterns of the institutions with less than university status, defies a composite picture. The characteristics of these institutions exhibit an even greater diversity than the community/junior colleges of the United States. During the past decade, the provinces have reemphasized their individuality of educational preference, further differentiating their provincial educational systems by establishing markedly different forms of postsecondary institutions. According to Campbell (1971), this is the consequence of a process of quiet evolution. "The national picture shows uneven growth of educational institutions, a certain lack of coordination between provinces, a remarkable diversity of functions, and in short an untidy state of affairs."

Neither this "untidy state of affairs" nor the wide range of institutional purpose within each provincial system has yet caused major articulation problems of the kind and magnitude identified in Chapter 3.

Some of the current provincial systems already contain the first signs of a possible tangled web of articulation and coordination,

127

but they can still be reasonably well handled by the individual institution. The demands of both social pressures and student numbers on provincial higher education systems have yet to reach the intensity found in many urban centers in the United States. The national enrollment figures[1] for publicly sponsored institutions of postsecondary education for 1969–1970 are as in Table 1. Private trade

Table 1

FULL-TIME STUDENTS IN TECHNICAL AND UNIVERSITY
TRANSFER COURSES IN CANADA

Technical courses	69,117	47,232 male
		21,885 female
Transfer programs	36,902	22,720 male
		14,182 female
	Total	106,019

schools enrolled 6,854 full-time and 6,294 part-time students, and private business schools enrolled 7,710 full-time and 8,350 part-time students. Diploma schools of nursing accounted for an additional 25,910 students.

The issues of articulation apply directly only to the 36,902 transfer students and to an undefined proportion of the 69,117 technical students who will want to continue their technical studies at the university level or to major in an academic subject. A province-by-province tabulation of the above full-time enrollment figures (Table 2) gives an idea of the magnitude of the articulation problem.

It is immediately apparent from the table that university transfer programs are offered in publicly supported community colleges in three provinces only. The small university transfer program output of Saskatchewan is the product of two privately operated postsecondary colleges.

Both the nature and magnitude of the Canadian articulation problem are still to be determined. The individual provinces exhibit ambivalence in their expressed philosophy of postsecondary education. Most provinces have not chosen between a system composed of two types of colleges (as exemplified by Ontario) and a single sys-

[1] All figures extracted from *Preliminary Statistics of Education 1969–1970.* Ottawa: Dominion Bureau of Statistics, Education Division, April, 1971.

Table 2
FULL-TIME STUDENTS IN TECHNICAL AND UNIVERSITY
TRANSFER COURSES IN CANADIAN PROVINCES

Province	Technical Courses	University Transfer Programs
Newfoundland	756	—
Prince Edward Island	96	—
Nova Scotia	794	—
New Brunswick	525	—
Quebec	20,919	31,359
Ontario	32,723	—
Manitoba	1,540	—
Saskatchewan	1,488	50
Alberta	6,727	1,838
British Columbia	3,549	3,655
Total	69,117	36,902

tem of higher education. The same indecision is shown in the difficulty of achieving comprehensive curricula in individual institutions and establishing communication between existing technical and vocational schools and those offering university transfer programs.

The sections that follow attempt to clarify and summarize the situation in each of the provinces by describing the system and identifying the unique problems or concerns of the province.

Alberta

Although the Colleges Act of 1969 made provision for the integration of all postsecondary nonuniversity education, the province presently has three subsystems (in addition to a number of private institutions with small enrollments): (1) Three agricultural and vocational colleges administered by the Department of Agriculture pursuant to the provisions of the Agricultural and Vocational Colleges Act. (2) Two provincial institutes of technology and art, a southern branch in Calgary (1916) and a northern and more recent (1963) one in Edmonton, administered directly by the Ministry of Education. (3) Six public colleges administered and controlled by the Alberta Colleges Commission, which has broad regulatory powers under the 1969 Colleges Act. The two institutes of technology and art have a full-time enrollment and annual operating budget approximately equal to or exceeding those of all the other colleges combined. This partly explains why the proposed integration remains to be developed.

Alberta has no legislation enforcing transferability. The permissive legislation of the Colleges Act, which allows for the establishment of affiliation agreements between institutions, is entirely unacceptable to the colleges.

Transfer agreements exist between individual colleges and university faculties (subject areas or departments), but the senior institutions accept only a limited number of the college courses. The limited and unsatisfactory nature of the transfer arrangements is best shown by students' statements that they can "get a better deal" from many good American universities than they can from the Alberta universities.

The Alberta colleges maintain that they should have the right to certify which students should be admitted to universities with appropriate advanced standing credit. The universities clearly wish to retain and use their veto power. There seem to be two possible evolutionary paths for the Alberta system to follow: the Institutes of technology and art and the agricultural and vocational colleges will be fully integrated into the public college system, establishing a single nonuniversity postsecondary system; or the ever-increasing financial demands of the various forms of postsecondary education will tend to force the development of a single system for all postsecondary/tertiary/higher education with the inherent danger of university dominance.

British Columbia

Under the legislation of the Public Schools Act and its 1970 amendments, a college may be established by a school district or group of districts after its citizens have passed a plebiscite (approval in principle) and a referendum (approval for specific local taxation for capital costs).

The Macdonald Report, *Higher Education in British Columbia and a Plan for the Future* (1962), recommended two-year colleges for designated communities throughout the province.

The colleges established during the mid and late 1960s were academically oriented, offering the first two years of university education and such other courses as required a high school diploma. A major goal, as exemplified by the establishment of Selkirk College (1965), was to make university education geographically accessible to an increasing proportion of the population. Since the province had already embarked upon a program of building postsecondary technical and regional vocational schools, it could be claimed that the nonacademic postsecondary student was already being accommodated.

An attempt has recently been made to create more comprehensive colleges by integrating the activities of existing vocational schools with the two-year colleges. The provincial-level administrative structure and the geographical separation of the institutions deter the effort to join these two forms of postsecondary education.

Authorized as they are under the Public Schools Act and financed by provincial/local cost sharing,[2] the affairs of the college are regulated by local school district administrations and trustees that dominate the college council membership.

In addition to the college council, two other groups share responsibility for the activities and governance of the colleges: the Division of Post-secondary Services (of the Department of Education) and the Academic Board for Higher Education. There are nine two-year colleges, one institute of technology and ten vocational schools currently in the public provincial system.

High school graduation from an academic-technical program is invariably the basic admission standard. Some colleges admit students without high school diplomas by examination and applicants with unusual experience and high abilities are given special consideration. Most community colleges are coeducational and comprehensive, in that liberal arts or general studies curricula and occupational programs are offered on the same campus. Remedial education, designed to prepare students for collegiate programs, has been started in at least one institution, the college of New Caledonia at Prince George. Adult education is offered in several of the new community colleges.

Transfer studies were initiated early in the development of the colleges. Two groups of transfer students from Vancouver Com-

---

[2] On a 60/40 percent split respectively for operating and capital (excluding site acquisition) costs. Tuition fees are included in the local 40 percent contribution.

munity College to the University of British Columbia in 1966 and 1967 were compared by Dennison and Jones. Their research (totaling approximately 360 transfers) indicated that the overall performance of the two groups was reasonably comparable. The authors also reported that the university performance of transfers was comparable to the university regulars. Transfers with incoming grade point averages of 2.5 and above actually did somewhat better than regulars. However the university regulars earned more first- and second-class grades. The authors concluded that 2.0 ought to become the minimum standard for university transfer admission. They further encouraged the interdependence among college and university faculties and administrators (Dennison and Jones, 1969).

Campbell describes and discusses four problems confronting the development and expansion of community college education. The issues, presented here in question form, relate directly to governance, financing and articulation:

(1) Which board or agency should govern the community colleges—a local college council or a division of the provincial government?

(2) To what extent should community colleges be locally financed?

(3) Should governance of the university and the community college systems be invested in a single board of higher education?

(4) What is the proper articulation balance among and between the several types of two-year colleges and the university to achieve the goal of maximum educational opportunity?

Manitoba

In December 1969 the three existing vocational centers in the province were renamed community colleges. It is not intended however that these renamed colleges offer university-level studies, but only that they satisfy the career and general education needs of the entire community.

Admission of community college students to the three universities of the province is done on an individual-merit basis. At the University of Manitoba, credits are granted where equivalence of training can be determined by the university.

The University of Winnipeg plans to establish two approaches to the transfer of credits: transfer of credits for equivalence of courses (this is now being done); and transfer of credit on a block basis for total programs taken at a community college whether or not the courses within the programs are equivalent to university courses.

The University of Winnipeg is further interested in developing hybrid degree programs; that is, courses to be selected from the University of Winnipeg and from the Red River Community College to build a unique degree program for the individual student.

Brandon University to date appears to have no specific policy on credit transfers from nonuniversity postsecondary institutions. Apparently this has not as yet become a problem.

Ontario

The dichotomy of secondary education established during the first half of the 1960s (see Figure 2) was capped by the Department of Education Amendment Act (1965), which established postsecondary colleges of applied arts and technology (CAAT). Beyond Grade Eight, the educational system is dual: the traditional

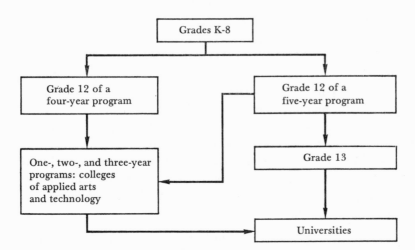

FIGURE 2. Public education in Ontario. (The fifteen universities presently have sufficient capacity to accommodate all qualified applicants, although not necessarily in the university program of their first choice.)

rigorous academic program which leads to the university-oriented Honour Graduation Diploma (Grade Thirteen); and a less rigorous high school program which offers a secondary school diploma not acceptable for university admission. The CAATs were created to provide career-oriented postsecondary education for secondary school graduates who do not qualify for admission to university.

Under the provisions of the original act and more recently under the Department of Colleges and Universities Act (1971), a CAAT may not offer university-level courses. Subject to the approval of the minister of education, a college board of governors may enter into an agreement with a university whereby the university can establish college programs leading to university degrees, certificates or diplomas. As of May 1972, there has been only one example of such an arrangement.

Movement of students from the CAATs to the university is possible only on an individual student basis. Universities are generally prepared to consider for admission to appropriate *second-year university* programs students who achieve high standing in a three-year program at a CAAT (three years of postsecondary education in a CAAT is equated with one year of university education). Some universities will expect first-class standing from students to be considered; others will expect high standing. At present just under 10 percent of CAAT graduates proceed to university education in this manner. Universities have further stated that they will consider for admission to an appropriate *first year* university program students who have achieved first-class or in some cases high standing in *two years* of nonuniversity postsecondary education.

The transfer of courses (or credits) between CAATs and universities simply does not occur as procedure. The individual CAAT student is admitted only on university judgment of individual merit based on past educational performance. As pressures and numbers increase, this individual merit form of decision making will no longer be workable.

Quebec

Although several other provinces (Ontario and British Columbia in particular) experienced a rapid evolution of their postsecondary education systems during the 1960s, the most radical and far-reaching development occurred in Quebec. Following the recommendation of the report of the Commission of Inquiry on Education in Quebec (the Parent Commission),[3] the General and Vocational Colleges Act (1967) established a new level of education between the existing high schools and universities—Colleges d'Enseignement General et Professionnel (CEGEP)/Colleges of General and Vocational Education. Students enter CEGEP after completion of secondary school grade eleven. They may then take the general two-year course for university preparation or may take the three-year technical-vocational program.

Prior to the passing of this act, college education for the French-speaking population was virtually a complete monopoly of the private classical college of Quebec. The classical colleges had status, tradition, and generally well-trained staffs, but they were strongly oriented toward an education suitable for a social elite. They were operated under private auspices, charged fees, and most of them were controlled by the church (Dupuis, 1971). The CEGEP were created for the following reasons, according to Dupuis:

To gather into a common legal and administrative framework all general and professional education given after high school and before university entrance.

To organize more efficiently all human and material resources in order to offer a program permitting a broad scope of options from humanities to technique.

To establish a clear, well-defined and workable liaison between secondary education and university.

To meet the growing demands for postsecondary education.

To ensure educational services throughout Quebec which will be of equivalent value.

To permit students a progressive orientation to their studies better adapted to their aptitudes and personalities.

[3] The Royal Commission Report, popularly called the Parent Report in honor of the commission chairman, Alphonse Marie Parent, was the landmark document influencing the official direction for the development of community colleges in Quebec.

To make available in all regions retraining and continuing education opportunities for the active labor force.

To offer all adults the kind of education they need in order to play an active and useful role in our society.

The organization of this level of education between the existing high schools and universities has produced a total system as in Figure 3.

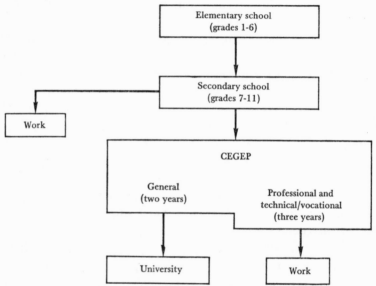

FIGURE 3.   Organization of education.

Since the system requires that all students attend a CEGEP for two years before becoming eligible for selection to the university, the latter is now firmly consolidated as an upper division and graduate institution in the Quebec system of higher education. The provincial government provides the entire operating budget of the public colleges and about 80 percent of it for the private colleges. There is no local taxation and no tuition. All other services including continuing education (usually referred to as community services in American community colleges) must be self-supporting.

Full-time students in both public and private institutions exceeded 72,000 in 1970–1971. In that year, approximately 58 percent were academic majors, some 40 percent semiprofessional and vocational majors, and 2 percent in teacher-training colleges (the latter are private institutions). About 90 percent of the full-time community college students are in the public colleges. It is interesting to note that women outnumber men in vocational training programs, suggesting the popularity of such curricula as nursing, home economics, and secretarial science.

As for the distribution of academic and vocational students, the Ministry of Education has set a goal of two-thirds vocational and one-third academic (general). The distribution for 1971–1972 is closer to a fifty-fifty balance. An ideal ratio of 70 percent vocational and 30 percent academic (general) was recommended for the Province in 1965 by the Royal Commission of Inquiry on Education in the Province of Quebec.

A significant feature of the new higher-education system is the establishment of upper-division universities. All but two universities are currently (1971–1972 midacademic year) upper-division and graduate only. This development, found in only a few of the fifty states, notably in Florida, should help to enhance the position of the Quebec community colleges.

Many community colleges are indirectly related to the Association of Canadian Community Colleges. It is anticipated that institutional membership will increase markedly in Quebec as the association strengthens its service across Canada.

Universities and community colleges are separate organizations with separate provincial governing boards. Once a diploma has been earned, showing that the student has completed his college work, he becomes eligible for entrance to a provincial university.

The nineteen member board of directors that governs the CEGEP colleges includes faculty members, representatives of student bodies, and parents. Five additional members are named from the general public to allow for maximum community participation (Campbell, 1971). This diversity of board membership assures a system of community-oriented colleges.

The chief administrator of a CEGEP college is called the principal; his chief assistant is usually an academic dean.

Counseling departments in general are severely understaffed, a situation that prevails in most American community colleges.

Part-time teachers are being recruited from industry to handle the rapidly expanding vocational curricula.

While the Ministry of Education wants eventually to provide more advanced educational opportunities for most eleventh-grade graduates, it can only approach that goal at present. Lack of facilities is the primary deterrent, but CEGEP colleges still admit between one-half to two-thirds of all applicants. In addition to the Grade Eleven diploma, above-average achievement students without diplomas are eligible for admission. Admission requirements are the same for both academic (general) and vocational divisions.

Most of the colleges have both the two-year academic (general)' curricula and three-year vocational programs. A student may change from general to vocational, or the reverse, at the beginning of any semester he chooses. The shift from vocational to general is obviously most easily accomplished in institutions that offer programs in both divisions, including the necessary university requirements. For example, an individual shifting from electronics to an electrical engineering major must complete the university prerequisite courses and have a college diploma. Typically he would be taking thirty-two or thirty-four courses as compared with the minimum twenty-eight. Engineers ordinarily remain two years at a community college and three years at a university.

Academic or general programs in community colleges are organized under five areas: applied science, paramedical science, human science, arts and letters, and administration. Paramedicine is included in the general college.

A student chooses his program from a college publication that gives course objectives, outlines, and bibliography. One section details core courses required of every student, regardless of major, both general and vocational. His total program consists of a minimum of twelve compulsory courses and twelve electives in one of three groups—science, human science, or arts and letters. From each group the student may select courses in three or four subjects. Four additional courses, making a total of twenty-eight, may be chosen from paramedical science and administration.

The core curriculum required of all students, general and vocational alike, is made up of four courses each in literature, philosophy or humanities, and physical education. While not all

CEGEP colleges offer every general and vocational program, all ostensibly offer the compulsory core courses.

At present about 85 percent of the Quebec university students transfer from the general divisions of CEGEP colleges and approximately 50 percent of all community college students are committed to transfer. An examination is provided by the provincial universities for students from other provinces.

Prerequisites are required in most major fields and the number varies widely. Little freedom for course selection for example is allowed in the paramedical major field. Establishing prerequisites (traditionally university prerogative) is one of the problems emerging from the development of a two-track higher education system in Quebec.

In addition to the problems of prerequisites and the inability to admit more Grade Eleven graduates, several other issues are defined and detailed by Campbell: limited facilities, administrative problems associated with the establishment of a new system, lack of employment opportunities for graduates of vocational programs, and need for innovative and nontraditional teaching techniques and administrative practices.

Educational leaders in Quebec have instituted fundamental changes in higher education. The establishment of a two-track college, the emphasis on community interaction, and the apparently flexible relationship between general and vocational programs offered in CEGEP colleges all have far-reaching implications for articulation. In these respects Quebec appears to be in the vanguard of the Canadian provinces.

Saskatchewan

The province currently has three nonuniversity postsecondary institutions, one private and two public. The public Saskatchewan Institute of Applied Arts and Sciences and the Saskatchewan Technical Institute are administered by the department of education without having boards of governors. In the past they have attempted to divide areas of study in order to meet the total needs of the province.

At present there is no legislation governing the transfer of credits from one postsecondary institution to another. Limited credits are given to students from the Institutes of Applied Arts and Sciences who register for programs on the university campus. In general course credits are recognized on a two-to-one basis; that is, two years of institute credits are equivalent to one year of university credits.

Legislation passed in February 1972 established a department of continuing education with responsibility for all post-high school education programs from courses taken simply for interest to the highly academic courses on the university campus. The major objective of the new department is to justify the total post-high school education program.

Atlantic Provinces

The provinces of this region maintain a nonuniversity postsecondary education system of many small special-purpose technological colleges or institutes and vocational schools as distinct from the comprehensive community college.

Recent developments such as the formation of the New Brunswick Higher Education Commission, the Prince Edward Island Commission on Postsecondary Education, and the Newfoundland Royal Commission on Education and Youth, together with their various reports and recommendations, all suggest that a more integrated and comprehensive system of postsecondary education is about to emerge.

Conclusion

Many of the problems and issues related to the smooth flow of students from the secondary level through higher (postsecondary or tertiary) education have yet to reach crisis intensity in the provinces of Canada. This is a result of two closely interwoven factors. The first factor is that the proportion of the population enrolled in higher education is low by United States figures. "The proportion of the eighteen- to twenty-four-year-old age group enrolled in colleges and universities increased from 4.2 percent in 1951–1952 to 10.1 percent in 1965–1966 and is expected to be 20.7 percent in

1975–1976 (Burn, 1971)." In the United States in 1965, 40 percent
of the eighteen- to twenty-one-year-old population was enrolled in
a degree credit program. For 1975, the projected enrollment is 49
percent. The second factor is that there has yet to emerge at either
the provincial or national level a clear-cut commitment to provide
higher education for all. Eligibility for higher education remains restricted on the doubtful premise that only a certain arbitrary proportion of the population deserves or can benefit from university
education.

As social pressures (particularly those of career education
and job entry) and student numbers mount, it will be interesting
to see if the quiet evolution of the provincial education systems becomes convergent or retains its dual course. Will the distinctly
binary system of Ontario be modified? Will the Colleges of Applied
Arts and Technology and the Colleges d'Enseignement Général et
Professionnel become more alike? Whatever evolves, articulation
problems and their temporary solutions will require a continuing
appraisal.

BURN, B. B. *Higher Education in Nine Countries: A Comparative Study
of Colleges and Universities Abroad.* New York: McGraw-Hill,
1971.

"College Canada," Association of Canadian Community Colleges.
November-December, 1970 and January-February, 1971.

CAMPBELL, G. *Community Colleges in Canada.* Toronto: Ryerson Press,
McGraw-Hill Ltd., 1971.

CAMPBELL, G. "Community Colleges in Canada: An Annotated Bibliography," Calgary, Alberta: Department of Educational Administration, The University of Calgary, 1972.

CAMPBELL, G. "The Community College in Canada," *Junior College
Journal,* November 1969.

Canadian Commission for the Community College. *Workshop on
Transferability and Exchange.* Vancouver, B.C. March 17–19,
1970.

"Community College Research in Western Canada: An Annotated
Bibliography," Edmonton: College Administration Project, The
University of Alberta, December, 1971.

DENNISON, J. D. AND JONES, G. *A Study of the Performance of Community College Transfer Students to the University of British*

Columbia. Vancouver, B.C.: University of British Columbia, 1969.

Department of Colleges and Universities Act 1971. Bill 98, Section 6, Subsection 5, Ontario, Canada, 1971.

Dominion Bureau of Statistics, Education Division. *Preliminary Statistics of Education, 1969–70.* Ottawa: Dominion Bureau of Statistics, April 1971.

Dominion Bureau of Statistics, Education Division. "Preliminary Statistics of Education," Ottawa, Canada (yearly).

DUPUIS, P. (in) *The Community College in Canada, Present Status/ Future Prospects.* Edmonton: College Administration Project, The University of Alberta, 1971.

PARENT, A. M. Royal Commission of Inquiry on Education. Quebec City, Quebec, Canada, 1965.

"Understanding Community Colleges," Edmonton: College Administration Project, The University of Alberta, May, 1972.

9

Directions and
Predictions

Articulation programs continuing through the seventies should result in widespread gains in the efficiency of junior–senior college student transfer. This prediction is based on plans established in the last two decades, styles described and analyzed in Part Two, statewide efforts, and plans involving individual senior institutions and groups of community colleges.

Three widely recognized and reported trends in junior college organization and administration have emerged: trends toward coordination by state boards or councils for community college education or for other or all public higher education; community college districts with two or more campuses; and the rapid development of comprehensive programs, particularly those in new careers directly associated with medicine, law, education, business, sociology, and many others that are likely to or have already expanded into baccalaureate degree curricula. All three trends, discussed in detail below, influence the development of articulation patterns. A fourth development, the upper-level university, has important articulation implications.

Coordination by State Boards

In recent years new state boards for public community colleges have been created in a number of states: Arizona, California, Connecticut, Florida, Illinois, Maryland, Massachusetts, Minnesota, and Washington. In other states—New Jersey, Ohio, Pennsylvania, and Virginia—community colleges were organized or reorganized under a single agency for higher education. Several states have placed their community colleges exclusively under the state university system: Alaska, Hawaii, Kentucky, Utah, and Wisconsin. In 1965 Arkansas named a Commission on Coordination of Higher Education Finance, which has become the State Community Junior College Board. Forty-three of the fifty states have state agencies responsible for coordination, supervision, or control of community colleges. Seventeen have centrally administered systems of community colleges (Wattenbarger and Sakaguchi, 1971).

As shown in reports from the fifty states (Part Two), most states have a committee, council, or board responsible for articulation, reflecting increasing state interest. Unless these agencies are broad based and student centered, the resulting articulation plans tend to be inflexible and arbitrary.

Statewide articulation committees have existed for many years in California, Florida, and Michigan, and are presently being formed in Connecticut, Iowa, Maryland, Missouri, New Jersey, North Carolina, and Virginia. In the latter state, a general education subcommittee of the Two-year/Four-year Articulation Advisory Committee held its first meeting in February 1970.

Multiinstitution Community College District

The multiinstitution community college district with two or more colleges or campuses is becoming increasingly popular, particularly in areas adjacent to densely populated centers. Related in an administrative way to the multiversity, multiunit community college districts—about fifty of them—are scattered throughout the country. Problems directly related to articulation are associated with this style of administration and organization.

Multicampus or college districts frequently suffer from poor communication systems, particularly between the central office staff and staff officers on the campuses. When articulation is centered in a district office, the process is likely to be somewhat slower and more cumbersome. Decentralization of the process to the various campuses promotes the individuality of the colleges but loses the values, economic and otherwise, of standardization of course descriptions for the entire district. The colleges must keep in mind that any articulation decision should be in the interest of the entire district.

Responsibility for articulation and instruction in multiunit community college districts is generally vaguely defined, if defined at all. Of the fifteen districts in California having two or more community colleges, only one—the Los Angeles Community College District—has an officer assigned specifically to articulation coordination. In several others this effort is divided between two or more offices; in most districts the responsibility remains unassigned. Articulation in a multiunit district is at best a district-level coordination activity.

Only a few California multiunit districts have officers for instruction. The Los Angeles, State Center, and Ventura Community College Districts list assistant superintendents for instruction. Coordination of instruction is divided among several officers in some districts, including Coast, North Orange County, and San Diego Community College Districts. Coordination of instruction at the central office is necessary to insure maximum efficiency and to avoid duplication of offerings (Kintzer, Jensen, and Hansen, 1969).

Comprehensive Programs and Curriculum Articulation

In the last decade two-year colleges throughout the country have become diversified institutions—increasing the number of occupational curricula while maintaining transfer programs. Two-year colleges have become community colleges in Hawaii, Iowa, North Carolina, and other states, having expanded their efforts to serve a diversified student body of all ages. Colleges in Alaska,

Kansas, Maryland, Massachusetts, New Jersey, Oklahoma, Pennsylvania, and Virginia are moving in that direction (Medsker and
Tillery, 1971).

Unfortunately curriculum diversification invariably complicates transfer relationships, confusing both the process and attitudes
toward articulation. When a community college initiates new occupational programs, it must face the problems associated with the
nontransferable status generally associated with such so-called career
programs. These include the possible loss of reputation as a worthy
academic institution. Articulation agreements, particularly with
major universities, therefore become more detailed and exacting.
Formerly recognized as transfer-versus-terminal education, the same
problem is currently recognized as liberal arts-versus-career education. The inclusion of all professional education in the career education concept further complicates the problems.

Although slow in coming, statewide studies of community
college education, some including an emphasis on articulation, are
underway in at least twenty states. Besides those described in Part
Two, guidelines for transfer are being written in Kansas, Maryland, North Dakota, and West Virginia. Some of the most recent
state efforts have unusual features: The Steering Committee in
New Jersey, which is helping to develop an articulation conference
type of organization; the North Carolina Joint Committee on College Transfer Students, which with the Community College Advisory Council is primarily responsible for an intricate system of
articulation study committees involving over a thousand educators;
and the Virginia Articulation Advisory Committee of the State
Council of Higher Education. All have published guidelines on
transfer of credits that were given final approval in 1969.

At least five states have university or state college offices
involved in the process of articulation with two-year colleges. The
Office of High School Relations (now including junior college
relations)' at Auburn University, Alabama, publishes a manual of
transfer guidelines to all Auburn curricula. In California a universitywide Office of Relations with Schools performs a liaison role
in course clearance and provides many other services to community
colleges. Offices of school relations in six of the nineteen California
state colleges have similar responsibilities. The Director of the Office

of Community College Affairs at the University of Iowa is statewide chairman of a group of subject-area articulation committees. The University of Michigan has for many years maintained a Bureau of School Services with responsibilities similar to those of the University of California universitywide office. An Assistant Director of Admissions for Community College Services is actually the university's liaison officer with the community colleges of Michigan. At the University of Washington, the Director of the Office of College Relations does the assigning of community college course transfer credit. The Western Washington State College Coordinator of College Relations is responsible for successful progress of community college students into and through his institution.

The University of Massachusetts-Amherst has recently created an Office of Transfer Affairs that performs a liaison role between students and departments.

An ombudsman for transfer students is the latest and most promising university contribution to facilitating smooth transfer. The Director of Inter-Institutional Relations at Florida Atlantic University (one of the upper division–graduate institutions in that state) actually serves in an ombudsman's role, hearing student complaints and working directly with the statewide Articulation Agreement Coordinating Committee on solutions.

The community college faculty member in the Arizona State University (Tempe) Center for the Study of Higher Education also serves as a kind of ombudsman. As trouble shooter for the community colleges on the university campus, he presents articulation problem cases before the Higher Education Coordinating Council. And the list of ombudsmen continues to grow.

Upper-Division University

A fourth development influencing the direction of articulation is the upper-division or upper-level university. A total of thirty-three are now found in at least seven states (Florida, Illinois, Indiana, Michigan, New York, Pennsylvania, and Texas). By definition the upper-level university is tied directly to the two-year college. Since these institutions are not in the business of lower-division education, they must rely heavily on community colleges for students.

The chief concern of an upper-level university is therefore its relationships with the community colleges in its region or state. In Florida, where this situation is best exemplified, upper-level universities have developed in close harmony with the two-year state colleges. Success is attributed to their willingness to respect the integrity of the community colleges. A provost of one of the colleges in the University of West Florida stated it this way: "We feel that the general education requirements are met if the student has his A.A. degree and we will not look back and reflect a D grade if this is a part of his earned A.A. degree. We accept the student and then build his program from that degree (Chaet, 1970)."

While the basic organization of the upper-division college eases the process of articulation with two-year colleges, the upper-level schools are not without their own status problems. They become both receiving and sending institutions and face the ignominy of being transition institutions between community colleges and universities. Some feel that the combination of upper-division and graduate programs is essential in avoiding the stigma of the middleman, the seemingly inescapable lot of the community college.

Upper-level university/community college articulation is not without problems. The chief concern is expressed in questions similar to those plaguing the traditional two- and four-year institution relationships: Are students adequately prepared for transferring to the upper-level university? Have they taken the right courses and enough of them to assure equal opportunity for success? Both institutions need to give a little to protect the transfer student.

Characteristics of Successful Agreements

Improvements in articulation are usually associated with better communication between segments of higher education and greater transfer flexibility of courses and credits. Statements related to institutional integrity often accompany announcements of plans to facilitate smoother and more efficient progress from junior to senior college.

Communication. Most of the states with community college statewide systems and also many senior institutions issue regular bulletins dealing with admission and transfer information, curricular developments, services and facilities, and other topics valuable to those contemplating transfer. Here are a few examples: *California Notes,* a monthly newsletter to schools and colleges from the Office of Relations with Schools, University of California. *Newsletter,* published monthly by the Office of Community College Affairs, University of Iowa. *Letters to Schools,* published bimonthly by the University of Michigan Bureau of School Services. *Higher Education in North Carolina,* a newsletter from the Board of Higher Education. *Information for College Transfers,* a booklet published annually by the University of Texas (Austin) Office of Admissions. *Memo to Schools,* a monthly publication issued by the University of Washington Office of New Student Services. *Hi U,* a monthly newsletter for high school counselors, teachers, and administrators, published by the Office of High School Relations at the University of Wisconsin. Other publications, primarily university- or regional association-sponsored booklets, provide transfer guidelines, updated course equivalent lists, and other vital information.

Every university in Florida annually publishes undergraduate degree program requirement booklets expressly for junior college counseling and instructional personnel. Each university in the state system provides such information to indicate the recommended lower-division and upper-division programs for every major. While universities in other states prepare similar documents, Florida is one of the few states, if not the only one, in which such detailed information is uniformly published by all public universities.

Other state university systems publish less detailed booklets. The University of California issues annually a *Prerequisites Bulletin* that provides much valuable information, but is by no means as complete as the Florida systemwide effort.

Statewide conferences are common in many states. Regular articulation conferences are held in California, Iowa, New Jersey, and North Carolina, where subject matter and service area (admissions, financial aids) committees hold discussions. Prior to Florida's commitment to a general-education formula, articulation problems were identified and task committees were organized. Statewide conferences were preceded by a statement on expected lower-division course requirements.

State universities with school or college relations offices or bureaus maintain close liaison with surrounding community colleges.

Institutional Integrity. Maintaining institutional integrity is crucial in the development of articulation agreements—the integrity of both the two- and four-year colleges. As presented in Chapter Four the Florida Formal Agreement Plan certifies the integrity of both associate and baccalaureate degree-granting institutions. In that document the two-year college is given responsibility for insuring that the associate degree indicates reasonable competence; the senior institution is responsible for assuring the transfer student an equal chance to complete work in his major.

Similar to the charge given higher education in Florida, the Oklahoma Agreement asserts: "After a public institution of higher learning in Oklahoma has developed and published its program of general education, the integrity of the program will be recognized by the other public institutions in Oklahoma. Once a student has been certified by such an institution as having completed satisfactorily its prescribed general education program culminated by an associate of arts or science degree, no other public institution of higher learning in Oklahoma to which he may be qualified to transfer will require any further lower-division general education courses in his program."

Statements suggesting a neutral guarantee of institutional integrity are specifically presented in other statewide guidelines or plans: (1) in sections 102–111 of the Illinois Junior College Act; (2) in the proposed Michigan statewide agreement; (3) in Phase Two of the New Jersey Master Plan for Higher Education; (4) in the Texas Core Curriculum for Public Junior Colleges; (5) in guidelines developed by the Virginia State Council of Higher Education; (6) in similar guidelines released by the Washington Interstate College Commission.

Flexibility. This is a third characteristic of effective articulation plans. Many of the rigidities common in past decades are presently being replaced by more tractable transfer allowances. Responses to the summer 1972 Inquiry on New and Unsolved Transfer Problem Areas from community college, university, and state officers in twenty-seven states and the results of other surveys support this premise.

One of the more tractable transfer allowances involves a wider selection of community college courses to satisfy senior institution graduation requirements or to apply as elective credit toward the baccalaureate. Although transfer of occupational curricula is still one of the major problems, credit for such work is acceptable in senior institutions in some twenty states. Such credit is most easily allowed by institutions that offer baccalaureate degrees in vocational-technical fields, such as several senior colleges and universities in North Carolina; or by schools preparing vocational-technical subject teachers, such as the University of Wisconsin-Stout. Led by several major universities or university systems, credit for occupational courses is applied at least as electives toward academic baccalaureates. The University of Washington and the California State University system illustrate this breakthrough. Reports of the acceptance of vocational-technical credits by universities in North and South Carolina, Illinois, Georgia, and New York were presented in Part Two. Senior institutions are also beginning to grant advanced-standing credit for work taken in technical schools sponsored by industry. The Massachusetts Institute of Technology among others will grant a full two years of credit to electronic technology graduates of RCA Institutes. Students at Control Data Institute get associate or baccalaureate degree credit at the University of Minnesota.

The credit arrangement worked out between the National Tool, Die, and Precision Machinery Association and the New York Institute of Technology is even more unusual. The institute will award up to one year of credit to those completing five year apprenticeships as tool and die makers (Burt, 1972). As suggested by Burt, wider use of the work of the Commission on Accreditation of Service Experiences (CASE) would undoubtedly hasten and strengthen the trend toward vocational-technical credit transfer. This commission, established by the American Council on Education in 1945 and endorsed by several national organizations, including the American Association of Community and Junior Colleges, published "A Guide to the Evaluation of Educational Experiences in the Armed Services" (1968). This document provides collegiate credit recommendations for about 8800 training programs connected with service schools. Greater use of the CASE system both speeds and simplifies the transfer process. In fact Burt has recommended that the commission be asked to explore the possibilities of developing specific articulation guidelines to be used by senior institutions in accepting community college vocational-technical programs.

Senior institutions, particularly the major universities, are generally cautious in receiving ethnic studies curricula, interdisciplinary programs, and other experimental efforts such as the black programs springing up so rapidly in community colleges. Again transfer problems are minimal where senior institutions are also experimenting. In several California state universities, full elective credit will be extended for ethnic studies courses and other experimental programs if they are listed as transferable in community college catalogs. The University of California system will accept a variety of experimental programs if the breakdown of subject matter covered and credit so assigned is given on transcripts or by other means. Several other universities will now assign at least elective credit to a variety of experimental courses if credits and grades for these are supplied by and are designated as transfer (collegiate) courses by community colleges. These include the University of Kansas, University of Massachusetts-Amherst, University of Michigan, Michigan State University, University of Nebraska, University of Nevada, New York State College of Agriculture and Life Sciences (Cornell University), Washington State University, University of Washington, universities in the Georgia and Oregon state systems, and most campuses of the University of Illinois. In Florida any credit course so designated by the community colleges becomes a transferable course.

There is increasing flexibility in transfer credit granted for units earned in advanced placement, CLEP (College Level Examination Program), external degree programs and for work experience equivalents. Granting of transfer credits in universities is still controlled by complex and highly technical bookkeeping systems sometimes called *the working rules*. Limitations remain fairly constant on the maximum number of credits a student may transfer (from 64 to 70 semester units and from 90 to 105 quarter units) and minimum grade point average for transfer admission (2.0). These limits were substantiated in the Scherer (1972) study. Considerable relaxation is seen, however, in the transferability of the amount and kind of credit earned through various examinations and to a lesser extent through work experience.

Credit or course exemptions or both are granted by a substantial number of senior institutions (more than nine hundred) through advanced placement examinations of the Council on College Level Examinations developed by the Educational Testing Service in cooperation with the College Entrance Examination Board. External programs, such as examinations for both associate and baccalaureate degrees offered by the New York State Board of Regents, are developing rapidly. Acceptable transfer limits on each of the c.l.e.p. battery of five general examinations are reported as scores of 500 or above and a similar level on each of the subject tests. Some institutions, including the University of California, will award as much as ten quarter credits for successful completion of the general tests and five (total) units for the subject examinations. Although twenty-nine subject examinations are currently available, only a few are extensively used. Most universities prefer to establish their own norms for acceptability rather than those recommended by the Council on College Level Examinations.

As indicated in the Scherer 1972 study, a large percentage of the nation's senior institutions grant c.l.e.p. credit. Use of these tests, particularly the c.l.e.p. general area examinations, has increased substantially in the armed services. They are now available free of charge to all servicemen and servicewomen and to dependents and overseas civilian personnel (Burt, 1972). This development alone will no doubt hasten flexible policy revisions in senior institutions for credit and course transfer and for admission to upper-division standing. The fact that the full associate in arts degree can now be taken through c.l.e.p. examinations gives clear indication of the potential of advance placement as a change catalyst.

The external degree program recently initiated by the New York State Board of Regents illustrates another trend. A significant feature of the New York Regents plan, through which either the associate or baccalaureate degree may be awarded, is the option of earning a portion of the degree credit at institutions or through c.l.e.p. outside the state (Burt, 1972). External degree-granting colleges and universities are developing in many sections of the country. Some are entirely external degree institutions, such as Thomas A. Edison College in New Jersey, which will administer the state program. Others have partial programs; Nova University in Florida has just announced an off-campus program for community college faculty leading to the Ed.D. degree.

The 1971 Report on Higher Education, commonly known as the Newman Report, hailed off-campus educational opportunities as "a different approach to making higher education more available and more stimulating for those unable to attend a college full-time." The report further claimed that the usefulness of these programs has been limited by the insistence of colleges and universities that they replicate traditional on-campus experiences.

Types of individuals who might benefit from this new approach to education are listed in the report: Young people who choose not to go to college or who choose to leave in the middle of their college program but who want to keep some contact with higher education; women who because of family responsibilities can manage only part-time classes; those who need new career training or upgrading in semiprofessional fields; urban ghetto residents and others who are not satisfied with conventional college routines.

These groups are now being served by comprehensive community colleges. While the Newman Report acknowledges this service, it tends to minimize the successes of many first-rate comprehensive community colleges. Chapter Twelve, which concentrates on the community college, is heavy with generalities that are strongly negative: "Already, community colleges have been converted in fact and in the public mind from community institutions to 'junior colleges'—kid brothers to the four-year institutions whose interests they serve."

Those who confine their reading on the comprehensive community college to this report perceive an overbalance of failure. The "junior college scenario" is vastly overplayed. While trends cited in the report must be faced honestly, the success column must also be recognized. (For a balanced view, the reader should study Medsker and Tillery, 1971, with particular attention to Chapter Four and the "Commentary" by Joseph P. Cosand.)

Newman realistically describes the external degree concept as one of the most exciting and yet dangerous movements in higher education today. "It is exciting because of the prospects for a more flexible and achievement-based system of higher education, but dangerous because of the possibility that it will result simply in investing fewer resources in students or providing them with cheapened degrees and a watered-down version of on-campus education" (Newman, 1972).

As initially recommended in the controversial but prestigious 1971 report, the federal government was encouraged to develop several experimental institutions called *regional examining universities*. These centers, empowered to administer examinations and to award college degrees, would presumably evaluate the desirability of expanding the concept of achievement-oriented testing. While the recommendation is a creative and stimulating one, considerable discussion is needed before the idea is implemented. Educators from a variety of traditional and nontraditional institutions should obviously be involved as the proposal takes shape.

Work experience equivalents are another example of flexibility as a characteristic of effective articulation. Work experience or work study programs are found in many senior institutions in such fields as education, business management, engineering, public administration, and other professional fields (Johnson, 1969). In recent years, similar programs have increased substantially in community colleges. Transfer of such credit however is negligible. Acceptability of work experience credits is generally confined to a few scattered senior colleges and universities such as the University of Cincinnati and Antioch College, both of which specialize in this type of education.

Developments in advanced placement and the growth of external degree programs have far-reaching implications for junior-senior college relationships. Implementation of both concepts in the form of the C.L.E.P. examinations, the New York Regents program, and external degree universities is already resulting in greater flexibility in articulation relationships. With increasing regularity senior colleges and universities are accepting the policies of community colleges on Advanced Placement, C.L.E.P., and Institutional Examinations. Credit is consistently granted in these areas if so recorded on the community college transcript. The number of students enrolling in advanced placement, independent study, and increasingly in external degree programs is a compelling force for change.

While the movement to simplify and liberalize admission

policies and procedures is a positive contribution in terms of service to students, the standardization of transfer courses inherent in the mass acceptance of c.l.e.p. examinations is a negative contribution. Uniformity and mediocrity could well result from an overemphasis on standardization.

Nontraditional programs are beginning to contribute to the financial problems of two- and four-year colleges alike. While as yet a minor factor in the drop of enrollments, the programs discussed in this section contribute to the attendance slowdown and to the financial crises now being experienced by higher education. Nevertheless pressure is mounting at the federal level, again through the work of the prestigious Newman Report and subsequent writing, for regional examining universities, college credit for life experiences, and other programmatic and structural changes in higher education.

The role of the community college as middleman in higher education is in part now being challenged by other organizations associated with business and industry. "Apology programs" in career education, developmental learning, continuing education, community services, and counseling and guidance will no longer suffice (Cosand, 1971).

Acceptance af Nonpunitive Grading Systems and D Grades

Nonpunitive Grading Systems. Caution and conservatism prevail in this area. Most of the respondents in the twenty-seven states reporting to the Inquiry on New and Unsolved Transfer Problem Areas indicated limited experience with pass-fail, credit-no-credit, and other adaptations of nonpunitive systems. Community colleges in North Carolina, Tennessee, Texas, and Virginia, among others, are evidently entirely graded. Several universities (Florida Atlantic, Hawaii, Washington State University, and California State University, Fullerton) would request a grading policy explanation or a statement of satisfactory completion. The University of Nevada among others accepts pass-fail courses when pass is at least a D. Public universities in Oregon may provisionally admit students with a preponderance of pass-fail credits and let them validate transfer by satisfactory university work. Some universities ignore nonpunitive grading systems, simply requiring a minimum number of transferable units with grades for admission. By ignoring the grading system of the transfer institution, a senior institution compounds the dilemma of transfer students.

Universities in Illinois are among the few developing grading policies that give students a variety of options. At Sangamon State University (one of the institutions in the Board of Regents system), a student may add statements on course success to his record to support or refute a professor's required statement. Students are also actively involved in course planning.

A performance-objective base is employed in curriculum development at Governor State University, one of the new institutions in the Board of Governor's System in Illinois. Transcripts show the learning modules as well as units of credit. Students agree to performance objectives and are awarded units as competencies are earned. Completed performance objectives might be reported on six or seven typed pages.

New universities, like new community colleges, are generally likely to initiate nontraditional policies. For the most part, however, community colleges are well ahead of senior institutions in initiating changes in grading systems. While the two-year college waits impatiently, it too faces the specter of the changing high school scene. The community college must make similar decisions on the acceptance or rejection of nonpunitive policies initiated by secondary schools. (For an authoritative study on the purposes and impact of grading, see Warren, 1971.)

D Grades. D grade transfer continues to be one of the most controversial issues. A scattering of senior institutions in nine of the twenty-seven states surveyed in the Inquiry on New and Unsolved Transfer Problem Areas reported acceptance of D grades and fewer had a system for repeating courses.

These examples illustrate the widespread changes lying immediately ahead. Some feel that forms of nonpunitive grading will soon entirely replace differential systems. Nevitt Sanford (quoted in Cohen, 1969) thinks that it would not be surprising if within the next few years distinguished undergraduate institutions were to give all their courses on a pass/fail basis. It will be recognized in time that what students need for their education is not grades. Cohen suggests further that the college of 1979 will have long since abandoned the differentiation between transfer and nontransfer courses as well as assigning grades. He predicts that criterion-reference testing rather than norm-reference examinations will be employed. "When a student has demonstrated his achievement of the objectives for a single unit, he is given credit for that unit and proceeds to the next."

Increased goal certainty is one product of nonpunitive grading systems. Under pass/fail, credit/no-credit arrangements students may be encouraged to attempt various subjects of interest before deciding on a major field. Complete expunging of a certain amount of credit from the community college transcript is a possibility if this advantage is to be tested.

If these predictions become reality, admission to the senior institution through its own normative examination system is a distinct possibility. If such a system is reinitiated, admissions will have completed the full cycle.

Relationship Between the Associate and Baccalaureate

The associate degree is widely recognized as a two-year college degree signifying completion generally of the first two years of the baccalaureate or a two-year program in an occupational curriculum. The basic issue in community college–senior college articulation is defining the purposes of the associate degree. What is meant by the proper kind and quality of associate degree education? Does this work adequately prepare the student for his major and upper-division courses? Is the associate degree a foundation for or a part of the baccalaureate?

While the early articulation agreements and first attempts at statewide plans were vague and indecisive in terms of lower- and upper-division relationships, current statewide proposals provide a clearer answer. The trend in articulation is toward the associate degree as a foundation for the baccalaureate.

Support for this direction is provided by a recent analysis of American degree structures developed by Spurr (1970) at the request of the Carnegie Commission on Higher Education. In his chapter on "The Associate's Degree," Spurr advocates general use of this degree. Requiring the associate degree en route to the baccalaureate, he reasons, would represent successful completion of the first phase of higher education in a community college, thereby serving as a prestige and recognition mechanism as well as a safety net for individual students. According to Spurr, "By bracketing together all who reach the two-year level with the associate's degree, whether on the completion of an academic or in a technical-vocational program, all successful students at this point will share the prestige and recognition and the sense of satisfaction and completion that comes from the possession of a college degree." Spurr also suggests that students be encouraged to move more rapidly through the degree requirements, with provisions made for early completion through Advanced Placement and other examinations.

Several dangers inherent in this plan were discussed at the end of Chapter Three. Perhaps the most critical is the temptation to segregate general education and specialization areas—the former in the community college, the latter in the senior institution.

The associate degree as Spurr further envisions it would not only be required en route to the baccalaureate but awarded routinely in four-year as well as two-year institutions. While meritorious in several respects, this plan would not retain the qualities that have made the associate degree the distinctive contribution of the two-year college. A certificate, an alternative suggested by Spurr, would preserve the community college degree and still mark the completion of lower-division work taken at the senior institution. Readmission for the baccalaureate would be mandatory and again, while commendable in certain respects, it could work to the disadvantage of students. The formal separation of lower and upper division as a strategy can be an inhibitor to flexibility, perhaps solving some paper problems but not people problems.

The Future

Mounting evidence indicates that the remainder of the decade will bring greater involvement in and control of two-year/four-year college articulation by state agencies. In most of the fifty states some type of statewide articulation authority—some voluntary and relatively informal, others mandated, even legislated—is working on systematizing policies. It is hoped that voluntary and cooperative efforts will wherever possible reverse the trend toward mandated articulation agreements and that emphasis will be placed on agreements providing equal opportunity for the transfer student in individual institutions. It is less than satisfactory to offer students access, but only on a statewide or systemwide basis. It is essential that all systems and plans provide for the movement of students vertically and horizontally to achieve their educational goals. Processes of articulation must center around the student.

A state organization for articulation may be necessary but should not be a substitute for a local committee. Each college and university must have its own organization. With California and Florida leading the way, collegiate institutions of all types are beginning to appoint articulation officers to represent them in statewide and regional systems, and many will expand their transfer counseling offices to include an articulation ombudsman.

The states currently without an articulation committee structure should be encouraged to develop an organization based on the Wattenbarger model presented in the Chapter Seven summary.

Improved computer technology will be more widely utilized to uncover transfer problem areas and develop answers from realistic data. Many states now have paper programs for handling credit-course transfer but few have mechanisms for solving personal problems—real barriers and imagined ones—which in fact prevent students from transferring and succeeding after transfer.

While private colleges and universities have in the past generally not shown particular interest in articulation planning, such concern is now evident. Representatives of private institutions should indeed be involved in statewide planning.

Core curriculum plans of articulation—a type of package acceptance in states where public higher education is managed by a university board of regents—will continue to serve widely scattered states, but will probably not experience widespread growth.

The increasing interest of the federal government in equal educational opportunity and the relationship of this concept to the entire spectrum of higher education is in general heralded as a positive force. Implications of the landmark legislation, The Education

Amendments Act of 1972 (Title Ten), and the influential and controversial Newman Report have already been discussed. Educators however are fearful that overstandardization and control would be an inevitable result of massive federal funding programs. The need for cooperative advanced planning and extended communication at the grass-roots level is critically important.

Interest in extending and broadening communication on the problems of two- and four-year college articulation has been informally expressed by officials in the U.S. Office of Education. A series of regional seminars or a national conference on a cooperative basis is a distinct possibility.

It is safe to predict that a total acceptance of the associate degree or a course package named by community colleges is very likely to develop rapidly in all corners of the nation and become commonplace by the end of the decade. As the pendulum swings toward greater two-year college authority to name and authorize lower-division transfer courses, it must be remembered that the baccalaureate degree is still going to be granted by the senior institution. The associate degree, as laudable as it is in its own right, may not be the appropriate lower-division preparation. The senior college or university must not be ignored.

Some crucial questions closely related to institutional integrity need to be answered: Is the primary purpose of the transfer program to approximate or duplicate the senior institution lower division in content, methodology, and background and preparation of faculty? Or should the program prepare students, by whatever means, to undertake upper-division work? Should general education be entirely confined to the lower division and subject-major work be taken only in the upper division? What courses are automatically transferred? Is the rationale for such judgments entirely satisfactory with both or all types of colleges? Above all, are transfer students realistically prepared for upper-division courses that in universities are likely to persist in traditional form? Can community college transfers compete with their university counterparts in specialized major fields?

Emphasis on career education discussed in Chapter Three, which accents continuous opportunities beginning in the pre-high school years, should help to redistribute students in occupational majors and ultimately into baccalaureate programs. Concerted efforts are badly needed to balance the two-plus-two-year system of the traditional liberal arts degree.

Much greater attention must be paid to high school–community college articulation. Activities outlined in Chapter Two suggest that this relationship is improving steadily.

Widespread changes in grading policies—including wholesale use of pass-fail/credit-no-credit "forgiveness" clauses, more extensive use of credit by examination, and advanced credit for work experience—may be expected in the immediate future. One of the most promising of the experimental procedures is multidimensional grading, in which teachers are required to evaluate types of performance crucial to success in a course, to define objectives on student achievement, and to interpret grading as a measurement of that achievement.

Articulation is a cooperative relationship. It is a process but also an attitude. The most effective articulation is invariably the result of a carefully developed partnership in education—a partnership in which high schools, community colleges, and senior institutions work together in the interest of the student.

Summary of Articulation Policies in the Fifty States

Alabama

Alabama Commission on Higher Education is responsible for articulation. Agreements exist only between individual institutions. A joint articulation committee may be created similar to the Florida task teams. Opposition to junior college education from senior institutions has eased considerably.

Alaska

Transfer students move from community colleges to the university according to policies of the Board of Regents. Comprehensive community colleges should develop in five years.

Arizona

Agreements differ somewhat among the universities. The Higher Education Coordinating Committee meets twice yearly to discuss transfer problems. The legislature strongly supports community college education. By 1980, eight out of ten lower-division students will be in community colleges. No vocational work transfers.

Arkansas

The community college system is just taking shape. Commission on Coordination of Educational Finance is the official articulation control agency. The university allows some vocational course transfer.

California

Articulation Conference Plan consisting of all educational segments and state government agencies remains the most powerful influence on articulation. University-wide Office of Relations with Schools processes curriculum transfer requests. Articulation with state universities and colleges remain on an individual basis. Governmental agencies may gain control of the voluntary Articulation Conference Organization. No vocational courses transfer to the university, a few can to the state university system.

Colorado

State Board for Community Colleges and Occupational Education is developing statewide articulation policies. The Colorado Association of Community and Junior Colleges is attempting to strengthen high school/community college articulation. A committee on junior/senior college relations from Colorado and Wyoming meets annually over articulation problems.

Connecticut

Comprehensive articulation is underway. The Commission on Higher Education has published a guidebook on transfer. Working agreements with state colleges and the university are established. Regional colleges are planned as comprehensive institutions.

Delaware

Reciprocal admission is maintained between the technical and community college and the university. Mutually acceptable policies and procedures are needed. The few transfer students are handled individually.

Florida

Details of the Florida Agreement, a statewide plan, are being perfected—including a new definition of general education and a clarification of vocational or occupational courses. An Articulation Coordinating Committee was established with the 1971 agreement. Education in Florida is recognized as a continuous process.

Georgia

The Georgia Core Curriculum provides areas of study rather than specific courses giving latitude to institutions. Junior colleges are a part of the state university system. Changes in an institution core curriculum must be approved by the transfer of Credit Committee and Council of Presidents. The concept as developed gives latitude to undecided students to make career decisions in the junior year. The sixty-hour core is difficult to complete in some fields.

Hawaii

The University Board of Regents is responsible for community colleges, and is also the State Board for Vocational Education. Subject-area articulation studies are underway. Although reciprocal admission is practiced throughout the system, transfer students must complete program requirements of receiving campuses.

Idaho

No important changes are expected. University teams still accredit junior colleges. The senior institution has final authority in course acceptance. Some vocational courses transfer. The State Board of Education is the coordinating agency.

Illinois

Illinois is nearing widespread acceptance of a statewide plan based upon legal authority stipulated in the master plan. Transfer guidelines have been adopted by the Board of Higher Education and a separate set for occupational students. A uniform and formalized system is being worked out. Northern Illinois University is the first to announce a junior standing policy. Two upper-division and first-year graduate universities have been established.

Indiana

No statewide articulation agreements exist. Availability of career-oriented programs in major universities hampers development of comprehensive community colleges.

Iowa

Community college districts with comprehensive programs are replacing area districts and vocational schools. The university accepts all transfer-designed courses. Technical courses do not transfer. Statewide transfer conferences are held annually. The Regents Committee on Educational Relations determines transfer credit policies.

Kansas

Transfer courses must be substantially equivalent to university courses. Planning reports of the Master Planning Commission will investigate articulation strategies.

Kentucky

Community colleges are a part of the university system and their credits are transferable without qualification. Technical courses are accepted, as are others not given on Lexington campus of the university on a course-by-course basis. Both university branches and community colleges are expanding in Kentucky.

Louisiana

Transfer students are admitted to the university system on a selective basis. A master plan is being developed by the Coordinating Council for Higher Education.

Maine

Transfer applications to the University of Maine are handled individually. A system of community colleges has been discussed but not implemented.

Maryland

Associate degree holders are given priority to transfer into upper-division work in the university and state colleges. Course transfer is granted on a course-by-course basis. No formal agreements have been perfected. The word *approximate* is used as a course acceptance guideline.

Massachusetts

The State Transfer Articulation Committee is actively engaged in developing statewide guidelines. The university now accepts associate degree graduates without question. University core requirements may also be completed in a regional college.

Michigan

A proposal has been developed by the state AACRAO group that would allow associate degree graduates to transfer automatically to upper-divisions of all four-year institutions with assurance that general education requirements have been completed. A voluntary articulation style has been practiced, but greater control by state agencies may be expected.

Minnesota

Articulation is arranged individually between institutions. Most state colleges accept the associate degree as fulfilling general education requirements. Local community college boards have little policy-making responsibility. The system is tightly centralized at the state level.

Mississippi

Junior college credits are accepted without question by the senior colleges and universities. A Junior-Senior College Conference annually reviews problems that occur in some university departments.

Missouri

Many state colleges in Missouri accept associate degrees without further evaluation. The university has so accepted associate degrees since 1971. Statewide articulation conferences are held regularly. The State Department of Education and the Commission on Higher Education serve a monitoring function.

Montana

Equivalent or similar transfer courses are uniformly accepted by the three University branches. Acceptance is based on the AACRAO publication. Technical courses transfer if approved by a dean or chairman.

Nebraska

The new two-year college system in Nebraska is called Technical Community Colleges. Although blanket approval of transfer courses has not occurred, approval in practice has been pretty well achieved. An AACRAO advisor's handbook is used in community colleges. The university holds articulation conferences.

Nevada

University equivalency is the transfer standard for community college course acceptance. The University of Nevada also uses the AACRAO grading listing. The University Chancellor's Articulation Committee has been formed.

New Hampshire

A comparable-course philosophy is the basis for university decisions on acceptance. The AACRAO document is also utilized. The state does not have a plan for creating a community college system.

New Jersey

The recent master plan sections on the necessity of accepting county college graduates into the public university system have erased much of the individual articulation effort. Agreements between state colleges and clusters of county colleges are being formed. The New Jersey Consortium on the Community College, a new organization, has recommended broad acceptance of the associate degree.

New Mexico

The AACRAO report is also used as a guide by the University of New Mexico and other public and private institutions. Pattern of credit acceptance is essentially the same as universities in most states—equivalency principle, sixty to sixty-six hour maximum.

New York

Students completing two-year programs are generally able to move into one of the 160 public and private senior institutions. Graduates are generally admitted as juniors. Four regional areas exist in which nearby community college graduates would be guaranteed admission to a senior college. The State University is taking the initiative. A plan to admit students to universities is being developed by the State Education Department.

North Carolina

The general education requirement issue has been greatly alleviated by the Joint Committee on College Transfer Students, which annually issues a policy booklet. Several public and private institutions including the university accept students and credits from technical institutions—general and technical education credits. The Joint Committee serves as a forum for articulation problems.

North Dakota

Formal transfer agreements have not been developed. The State Board of Higher Education has adopted guidelines.

Ohio

Transfer into the university system is handled on an individual basis. While no specific plan exists, the Board of Regents has appointed an advisory committee to deal with course acceptance. As in most states the question of technical course transfer is the most difficult problem. The master plan calls for increased attention to articulation.

Oklahoma

The master plan published in July 1971 endorses a system of comprehensive two-year colleges. The 1972 general education agreement (which does not include private institutions) was also recommended in the master plan and is now being implemented. How to handle technical courses is again the critical problem.

Oregon

The State System Community College Committee annually issues a list of recommended transfer programs. Students following a specified program will not lose time or transfer credit. Full recognition of the associate degree (in fulfilling all lower-division general education requirements) is under consideration by senior institution faculties. Technical courses in many fields are accepted, particularly by Oregon Technical Institute.

Pennsylvania

The Department of Education's Bureau of Planning recently created ten regions for higher education planning and articulation development. All institutions within a region would be served by a regional committee. While statewide policies do not exist, guidelines are being considered. Equal treatment of transfers and natives is a basic consideration under discussion. Most colleges accept the usual sixty transfer units and some accept technical education credits. Automatic transfer to the university is not assured.

Rhode Island

The university restricts transfers to "space available." Transfer numbers have been increased to about 500 per year. Course acceptance from Rhode Island Junior College is offered on an equivalent basis.

South Carolina

South Carolina has no public junior colleges. College-parallel programs are provided locally by regional campuses or branches of the State University or Clemson University. Under a legislative mandate, a State Committee is devising a plan for comprehensive community colleges.

South Dakota

South Dakota recently established its first junior college. This public institution and the two private schools are accredited by the university for course transfer purposes. The Post-High School Coordinating Council deals with articulation problems.

Tennessee

Advanced standing admissions are handled on an individual basis. The university is apparently recognizing its commitment to transfer students by creating a Committee on Articulation that submitted guidelines for improving communication. A master plan for the state is being prepared.

Texas

The Texas Modified Core Curriculum Articulation Plan was adopted in 1966. Interpreting the phrase *freely transferable* used in enabling legislation, transferable courses in the community college core in a particular field must apply toward senior college requirements. The core curriculum refers to general education and major field work at a community college in Texas.

Utah

Associate degree graduates are considered to have fulfilled general education requirements of the university. Transfer numbers are small. Most transfers are placed immediately in major fields. Utah State University has developed a new general education program and accepts such credits taken in other institutions within the state system.

Vermont

The Vermont Regional Community College was created in 1970. Technical curricula in this new institution are developed in close coordination with the Vermont Technical Institute. Transfers are small in number. A board for all of higher education is contemplated.

Virginia

Guidelines developed by the Articulation Advisory Committee of the State Council of Higher Education serve as transfer policy. Core courses are basic to all associate degree curricula. Community college courses are generally accepted on an equivalency basis. Technical courses may be used as electives or apply directly to technically oriented B.A. programs.

Washington

Washington has an unusually good environment, political and otherwise, for settling articulation problems. All senior institutions have added flexibility to transfer regulations. Washington State University is the first to grant full recognition to the associate degree. Others are moving rapidly toward unquestioned acceptance, as outlined by the Inter-College Relations Commission.

West Virginia

West Virginia has two comprehensive community colleges under a single State Board of Regents. Full transferability of college-parallel credit from a community college is expected to develop. The State Plan for Higher Education has been recently published and includes the basic transfer policy of the board.

Wisconsin

Transfer and technical education are developed in Wisconsin by separate groups of institutions. *Community* and *junior* colleges, by name, are not found in the state. The University of Wisconsin Center System is responsible for solving transfer problems. The Wisconsin AACRAO organization also considers articulation problems. Most technical courses are nontransferable.

Wyoming

A committee of Wyoming and Colorado educators meets annually over articulation problems. Transfer student numbers, while still small, are beginning to increase rapidly. The Wyoming Higher Education Council represents all of higher education, and seeks better coordination between the segments.

Bibliography

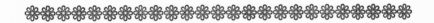

American Association of Collegiate Registrars and Admissions Officers. *The AACRAO Survey of Grading Policies in Member Institutions.* Report of the Ad Hoc Committee to Survey Grading Policies in Member Institutions. Washington, D.C. 1971.

American Association of Collegiate Registrars and Admissions Officers. *Report of Credit Given by Educational Institutions.* Washington, D.C.: 1972.

ASHBY, E. *Any Person, Any Study.* New York: McGraw-Hill, 1971.

BIRD, G. V. "Preparation for Advanced Study." In *The Public Junior College.* Fifty-Fifth Yearbook of the National Society for the Study of Education. Chicago: National Society for the Study of Education, 1956.

BREUDER, R. *A Statewide Study: Identified Problems of International Students Enrolled in Community/Junior Colleges in Florida.* Tallahassee: Department of Higher Education, May 1972.

BURT, S. M. *The Dilemma of the College Undergraduate Transfer Student: Implications for National Policy Relating to Higher Education.* Washington, D.C.: Federal Interagency Committee on Education Task Force on Transfer of Credits in Higher Education, 1972.

Carnegie Commission on Higher Education. *Quality and Equality: New Levels of Federal Responsibility for Higher Education.* New York: McGraw-Hill, 1968.

Carnegie Commission on Higher Education. *A Chance to Learn: An Action Agenda for Equal Opportunity in Higher Education.* Berkeley, Calif.: 1970a.

Carnegie Commission on Higher Education. *The Open-Door Colleges: Policies for Community Colleges.* New York: McGraw-Hill, 1970b.

Carnegie Commission on Higher Education. *The Capitol and the Campus.* New York: McGraw-Hill, 1971a.

Carnegie Commission on Higher Education. *New Students and New Places.* New York: McGraw-Hill, 1971b.

Carnegie Commission on Higher Education. *The Fourth Revolution: Instructional Technology in Higher Education.* New York: McGraw-Hill, 1972.

CHAET, A. B. "The First Six Years." *Proceedings of the International Conference on the Upper-Level University/Junior College Partnership.* Pensacola: University of West Florida, June 1970.

COHEN, A. M. *Dateline '79: Heretical Concepts for the Community College.* Beverly Hills, Calif.: Glencoe, 1969.

COHEN, A. M. AND ASSOCIATES. *A Constant Variable.* San Francisco: Jossey-Bass, 1971.

COREY, J. F. *Articulation Among Various Levels of Education Beyond the High School in North Carolina.* Raleigh: State Board of Higher Education, 1971.

CORSON, J. J. *Governance of Colleges and Universities.* New York: McGraw-Hill, 1960.

COSAND, J. P. "An Equal Opportunity to the Transfer Student." *The Transfer of Credits from Junior Colleges to Senior Colleges.* Report of the Fifth Annual Missouri Valley Conference on Cooperation Between Junior and Senior Colleges, Central Missouri College, April 1970.

COSAND, J. P. "Commentary" (see Medsker and Tillery) 1971.

CROSS, K. P. *The Junior College Student: A Research Description.* Princeton: Educational Testing Service, 1968.

CROSS, K. P. *Beyond the Open Door.* San Francisco: Jossey-Bass, 1971.

DARNES, B. R. "Problems to Be Encountered by a No 'F' Grading Policy." (Unpublished paper) April 1971.

DARNES, G. R. "Articulation in Illinois." (Unpublished paper) March 1972.

Education Commission of the States. *Community and Junior Colleges in Perspective: Report of the Task Force on Community and Junior Colleges,* Denver: April 1971.

ELDERSVELD, A. M. "Curriculum Master-Planning in the Virginia Community College System." (Unpublished paper) March 1972.

FERRIN, R. I. *A Decade of Change in Free-access Higher Education.* New York: College Entrance Examination Board, 1971.

GILES, F. T. AND WIESE, H. *Mobility of Undergraduate College Students Between Washington Colleges and Universities, Autumn, 1970.* Seattle: University of Washington, March 1971.

GLEAZER, E. J., JR. *This is the Community College.* Boston: Houghton-Mifflin, 1968.

GOOD, C. V. *Dictionary of Education* (Second Edition) New York: McGraw-Hill, 1959.

HENDERSON, L. "Closing Address." *Proceedings of the International Conference on the Upper-Level University/Junior College Partnership.* Pensacola: The University of West Florida, June 1970.

HILLS, J. R. "Transfer Shock: The Academic Performance of the Junior College Transfer," *The Journal of Experimental Education,* Spring 1965.

HODGKINSON, H. "Reflections on the Newman Commission." *Change.* May 6, 1972.

HURLBURT, A. S. *State Master Plans for Community Colleges.* Washington, D.C.: American Association of Junior Colleges/ERIC Clearinghouse for Junior Colleges, Monograph, No. 8, 1969.

JOHNSON, B. L. *Islands of Innovation Expanding: Changes in the Community College.* Beverly Hills: Glencoe Press, 1969.

Joint Committee on Junior and Senior Colleges. *Guidelines for Improving Articulation Between Junior and Senior Colleges.* Washington, D.C.: American Council on Education, 1966.

KINTZER, F. C. "Admission of Students to California Public Junior Colleges Who Are in Academic Difficulty at the University of California." *College and University,* Winter 1966.

KINTZER, F. C. "Articulation Is an Opportunity." *Junior College Journal.* April 1967a.

KINTZER, F. C. "Profile of an Ideal Community Junior College." *College and University.* Summer 1967b.

KINTZER, F. C. "The California Plan of Articulation: Recent Developments." *College and University.* Summer 1968a.

KINTZER, F. C. "The California Plan of Articulation." *College and University.* Winter 1968b.

KINTZER, F. C. *Nationwide Pilot Study of Articulation.* Topical Paper No. 15. Los Angeles: ERIC Clearinghouse for Junior Colleges, UCLA, 1970.

KINTZER, F. C. "Junior College-Senior College Articulation in the '70's." *College and University,* Summer 1971.

KINTZER, F. C. "From High School to Community College: A Vital Link in the Articulation Process." *ERIC Junior College Research Review,* June 1972.

KINTZER, F. C., JENSEN, A. M., AND HANSEN, J. S. *The Multi-Institution Junior College District.* Washington, D.C.: Monograph No. 7, ERIC Clearinghouse for Junior Colleges/American Association of Junior Colleges, 1969.

KNOELL, D. M., AND MEDSKER, L. L., *Articulation Between Two-Year and Four-Year Colleges.* Berkeley: Center for the Study of Higher Education, University of California, 1964a.

KNOELL, D. M. AND MEDSKER, L. L. *Factors Affecting Performance of Transfer Students from Two- to Four-Year Colleges: With Implications for Coordination and Articulation.* Berkeley: University of California, 1964b.

KNOELL, D. M. AND MEDSKER, L. L. *From Junior to Senior College.* Washington, D.C.: American Council on Education, 1965.

LEE, E. C. AND BOWEN, F. M. *The Multicampus University.* New York: McGraw-Hill, 1971.

LEWIS, I. G. "Aspects of Articulation." (Unpublished report) Pasadena City College, Calif., 1970.

LEWIS, J. R., JR. *Articulation Project,* Giles County Vocational School, Pearlsburg, Va., May 1972.

LOMBARDI, J. "Moratorium on New Junior Colleges." *ERIC Junior College Research Review,* May 1972.

LONG, E. T. *School Relations in the California State Colleges: A Report to the Joint Legislative Budget Committee.* The California State Colleges, June 1969.

MC CONNELL, T. R. (in KNOELL, D. M. AND MEDSKER, L. L.) (Part IV). *Factors Affecting Performance of Transfer Students from Two- to Four-Year Colleges: With Implications for Coordination and Articulation.* Berkeley: University of California, 1964.

MARTORANA, S. V. "Developments in State-Level Governance." *Junior College Journal.* 1969.

MEDSKER, L. L. *The Junior College: Progress and Prospect.* New York: McGraw-Hill, 1960.

MEDSKER, L. L. AND TILLERY, D. *Breaking the Access Barriers: A Profile of Two-Year Colleges.* New York: McGraw-Hill, 1971.

MUIRHEAD, P. P. "Community-Junior Colleges and Universities Plan for Career Education." *Community Junior Colleges and Universities: Partners in Higher Education.* Los Angeles: Community College Leadership Program, 1973.

National Center for Educational Statistics. "Fall Enrollments in Higher Education: Supplementary Information, Summary Data, 1970." Washington, D.C.: U. S. Department of Health, Education, and Welfare, 1970.

NELSON, J. H. "Do Junior College Transfers Make the Grade?" *Perspectives on the Community-Junior College.* New York: Appleton-Century-Crofts, 1971.

NEWMAN, F. (and Associates). *Report on Higher Education.* Washington, D.C.: U. S. Department of Health, Education, and Welfare. U. S. Government Printing Office, 1971.

NEWMAN, F. "A Review of the Second Newman Report." *Change.* May 6, 1972.

NICHOLSON, D. H. *A Step Ahead.* Murfreesboro, N.C.: Chowan College, 1971.

NICKENS, J. M. "Transfer Shock or Transfer Ecstacy?" (Unpublished paper) University of Florida, College of Education, 1972.

OGILVIE, W. L. AND RAINES, M. R. *Perspectives on the Community-Junior College: Selected Readings.* New York: Appleton-Century-Crofts, 1971.

PLUSCH, J. O. *A Study of the Employment Problems and Prospects of a Selected Group of Male Occupationally-Oriented High School Graduates.* (Unpublished dissertation) Los Angeles: University of California, 1967.

RICHARDSON, R. C., JR., BLOCKER, C. E., AND BENDER, L. W. *Governance for the Two-Year College.* Englewood Cliffs, N.J.: Prentice-Hall, 1972.

ROBSON, J. W. "Criteria of the Acceptability of Courses." (Unpublished report) Los Angeles: University of California, October 1952.

San Francisco Unified School District. "A High School Student and Teacher Counselor Project at the City College of San Francisco." 1968.

SCHERER, P. L. "Junior-Senior College Articulation." University of

California, Santa Barbara. *College and University.* Summer 1972.

SCHULTZ, R. E. "Articulation in Undergraduate Higher Education: Some Problems and Some Recommendations Related to the Junior College." *Perspectives on the Community-Junior College.* New York: Appleton-Century-Crofts, 1971.

SEYMOUR, W. R. AND COLLIS, R. "The Problem of Junior College Transfer Students: A Review of On-Campus Research." (Extra Divisional Administration Report No. 4) Columbia: University of Missouri, 1968.

SIMONDS, H. E. "Report on the Los Angeles Colleges—Secondary Articulation of Occupational Education Programs." Los Angeles School District, 1971.

SMITH, A. K. "Bridging the Gap—High School to Community College." *Junior College Journal,* February 1970.

SPINDT, H. A. "Relations of the Junior Colleges and the University of California." (Unpublished report) Berkeley: University of California, October 1954.

SPURR, S. H. *Academic Degree Structures: Innovative Approaches.* New York: McGraw-Hill, 1970.

"State Colleges Alter Transfer Requirements." *The Courier.* Los Angeles Community College District, December 1971.

STRONG, E. W. "Acceptability of Courses for Letters and Science Credit." (Unpublished report) Berkeley: University of California, October 1951.

THORNTON, J. W., JR. *The Community Junior College* (Second Edition) New York: John Wiley, 1966.

TRENT, J. W., AND MEDSKER, L. L., *Beyond High School.* San Francisco: Jossey-Bass, 1968.

WARREN, J. R., *College Grading Practices: An Overview.* Washington, D.C.: George Washington University. ERIC Clearinghouse on Higher Education, March 1971.

WATTENBARGER, J. L. "Foreword." *Guidelines for Improving Articulation Between Junior and Senior Colleges.* Washington, D.C.: American Council on Education, 1966.

WATTENBARGER, J. L. "State Control of Junior Colleges." *Junior College Journal,* May 1968.

WATTENBARGER, J. L. "Articulation with High Schools, Colleges and Universities." *Student Development Programs in the Community Junior College.* Englewood Cliffs, N.J.: Prentice-Hall, 1972.

WATTENBARGER, J. L. AND SAKAGUCHI, M. *State Level Boards for Community-Junior Colleges: Patterns of Control and Coordination.* Gainesville: Institute of Higher Education, University of Florida, 1971.

WILLINGHAM, W. W. *The No. 2 Access Problem: Transfer to the Upper Division.* American Association of Higher Education Monograph Series. Washington, D.C.: ERIC Clearinghouse for Higher Education, George Washington University, 1972.

WILLINGHAM, W. W. AND FINDIKYAN, N. *Patterns of Admission for Transfer Students.* New York: College Entrance Examination Board, 1969.

WILSON, G. C. "The Impact of Transfer Admissions on the Next Decade." *College and University.* Spring 1970.

YARRINGTON, R. (Editor). *Junior Colleges: 50 States/50 Years.* Washington, D.C.: American Association of Junior Colleges, 1969.

Index

A

Academic record forms, 60

Accreditation: role of, 23–24, 29, 47, 55, 60–61, 126; of technical schools, 60; by university, 75

Admissions, transfer: policies on, 8, 27–29, 44, 49–50, 54–56, 59–60, 62, 65, 78, 97–98; priorities for, 49, 79, 93, 98. *See also* individual states

Adult education, 18, 60, 72, 85, 136

Agreements, articulation: characteristics of successful, 148–156; communication in, 148–149; flexibility in, 150–156; institutional integrity in, 150; typology of, 33–34, 52. *See also* Articulation; individual states

Alabama, 107–108, 163

Alaska, 108, 163

Alberta, 129–130

American Association of Collegiate Registrars and Admissions Officers, 5, 70, 116–117, 123–124, 126, 168; guidelines of, 124; influence of, 126; *Report of Credit Given by Educational Institutions* by, 116–117, 126, 168–169; study by, 10–11

American Association of Junior Colleges, 5, 124, 151

American Council on Education, 6, 151

ANDERSON, K. E., 113

Antioch College, 155

Appalachian State University, 54, 56

Appeals system, 126

Application forms, uniform, 82

Arizona: articulation in, 73–76; occupational programs in, 75–76; registrars in, 74; summary of, 163; varying policies in, 74–75

Arizona State University, 74–75, 147

Arkansas, 108–109, 164

Armed services' courses, 151

Articulation: and accreditation, 23–24, 29, 47, 55, 60–61, 126; administration of, 2; agreements on, 146–156; attitude toward, 2, 25; barriers to, 27–29; bookkeeping problems in, 28, 152; books on, 11; Canadian, 124–142; committee structure for, 44, 160; communication about, 20–21, 29, 148–149; community college knowledge about, 11; complexity of, 9; cooperative planning of, 2; and curriculum, 11–14, 83, 103–105; definition of, 1; in district office, 145; "downward," 17–25; faculty views on, 26; federal role in, 160–161; formal and legal, 35–51; guidelines for, 8–10, 146; high school–community college, 5, 17–25, 157; history of, 5–16; implementation of, 10, 47; by individual institutions, 160; on individual student basis, 107, 123; and institutional integrity, 13, 105, 150; institutional-system type of, 52, 66–95; Knoell-Medsker study of, 6–7; by local committees, 160; model for, 124–125; obligations of partners in, 14, 145; philosophical problems in, 28, 100; predictions about, 143–162; pressure for, 124; principles of, 39, 43, 48, 64–65, 78–79, 88–89; responsibility for, 145; senior institution–community college, 26–31; state-agency type of, 52–66, 159; statewide committees on, 144, 160; student-centered, 160; studies of, 6–10, 14–16; typology of agreements on, 33–34, 52; with upper-division institutions, 148; voluntary, 43, 96–106, 160; Wattenbarger model of, 125, 160. See also Conferences; Credit; individual states; Publications on transfer; Transfer

Associate degree: automatic acceptance of, 10, 13, 65, 80, 95, 148, 161; awarded by senior institution, 159; and baccalaureate, 30, 158–159, 161; definition of, 93, 158; by examination, 153; general education requirements for, 31; integrity of, 150; package transfer of, 94, 161; problems of, 31, 161; in science/technology, 53–55, 63, 89–90, 110; specialized, 87; as transfer requirement, 27, 30–31, 50, 58, 66, 78, 80, 83, 91–92, 161

Association of American Colleges, 5, 124

Atlantic Provinces, 140
Auburn University, 146

B

Baccalaureate degree: by examination, 153; relation to associate degree of, 30, 158–159, 161; senior institution control over, 28, 97; in technology, 53–55, 89

Behavioral objectives, 111, 157, 162
Bellevue Community College, 23
BIRD, G. V., 15, 30
Black studies, 152
Boise College, 112
Bookkeeping procedures, 8, 28, 152
British Columbia, 130–132
Bucknell University, 90
Buffalo, State University of New York at, 86
BURN, B. B., 141
BURT, S. M., 151, 153

C

Calendar, academic, 36, 40
California: articulation in, 10, 21, 96–102; associate degree in, 100–101; conference plan in, 21, 97; experimental curricula in, 152; high school–community college articulation in, 19–21; history of articulation in, 12; master plan in, 97; policies of state universities in, 99–100; policies of University of, 98–99; summary of, 165; transfer guidelines in, 97–98

California, University of, 12–13, 98–99, 146–147, 149

California State University, 151
Caminetti Act, 12
CAMPBELL, G., 127, 132, 137, 139
Canada, 127–142; admissions policy in, 138; adult education in, 131, 136; communication problems in, 129; community college association in, 137; community college development problems in, 132; comprehensive curricula in, 129, 131; continuing education in, 140; dual education system in, 133; enroll-

ments in, 128–129, 134, 136–137, 140; geographical distribution in, 130; Parent report in, 135; remedial education in, 131; studies on transfer in, 131–132; technical and vocational schools in, 128–129, 131, 133, 139; transfer courses in, 128–129; and United States schools, 130. *See also* individual provinces

Capstone program, 85

Career education, 86; articulation of, 25, 85; definition of, 24–25; in high school, 18; nontransferability of, 146; redistribution of students with, 161. *See also* Vocational/ technical courses

CASE, 151

Center for Study of Higher Education, Berkeley, 6

Central Washington State College, 91, 94

CHAET, A. B., 148

Chowan College, 53

Cincinnati, University of, 155

City College of San Francisco, 19

City University of New York, 22, 84, 86

COHEN, A. M., 11, 157, 158

College Level Examination Program (CLEP), 79, 82, 152–153

Colleges. *See* Senior institutions

Colorado, 21, 109–110, 164

Commission on Accreditation of Service Experiences, 151

Committee structure, articulation, 160

Communication problems, 11, 20–21, 29, 148–149

Community colleges: administration of, 143; admissions policy of, 1, 4, 29; adult education by, 60; attendance slowdown in, 156; caring by, 4; communication problems among, 11, 145; community service by, 60; complaints about senior institutions by, 26–27; comprehensive, 145–147, 154; as confidence-givers, 2–3; counseling by, 60; curricula in, 3, 11–14, 143; designation of transfer courses by, 161; districts for, 18;

enrollments in, 56, 76; financial problems of, 156; general education versus major work in, 88; geographical reach of, 64, 131; governance of, 143–144; and high school articulation, 17–25; independence of, 30; inner city, 29; lack of knowledge about articulation in, 11; multicampus, 143–145; nonpunitive grading in, 156–157; nontraditional students in, 154; nontransfer programs in, 59, 75; occupational programs in, 75; quality of education in, 14, 79, 83, 95; remedial education in, 2, 75; role of, 1–2, 4, 7, 154; as second-chance institutions, 8–9; and senior institution articulation, 26–31; state-board coordination of, 144; under state university systems, 144; statewide studies of, 146; students at, 4; transfer into, 2–3, 47–48; trends in organization of, 143; urban, 29; upper-division courses in, 59, 74–75; as vocational schools, 97, 108

Comprehensive programs, 145–147

Computers, use of, 160

Conferences, statewide, 34, 47, 53, 63, 81, 86, 88, 91, 116, 146; summary of, 149, 160

Connecticut, 110, 164

COSAND, J. P., 154

Council on College Level Exams, 153

Counseling, 9, 82, 105; in high school–community college articulation, 19; importance of, 4; inadequacy of, 7, 137; by students, 19

Courses, community college: college-parallel (transfer), 12–13, 26, 45, 56, 61, 67, 69, 74, 85, 108; designated as transferable by community colleges, 152; development of, 30; equivalent, 13, 66, 70, 114; examined by senior institution, 27, 48; remedial, 75; sequential, 68–69; state approval of, 102; substandard, 28, 56. *See also* Credit; Curriculum; individual states; Vocational/ technical courses

Credit: authority for granting, 27–28, 44, 66, 71, 73–74, 89, 98, 102; elective, 45, 48, 79, 89, 99, 151; expunging of, 158; for external degree program, 152; guidelines for transfer of, 12–13, 26–28, 41–42, 44–45, 47, 62, 64–65, 67–68, 78–79, 88–89; for independent study, 64, 79; maximum transferable, 27, 45, 50, 62, 69, 70–75, 77–78, 93, 112, 152; nontransferable, 67, 75, 77, 90, 94, 104, 158; unlimited transfer of, 67, 123; for work experience, 64, 152, 155. *See also* Examination; individual states; Vocational/technical courses

CROSS, K. P., 16

Curriculum: acceptability of experimental, 152; articulation of, 11–14, 83, 103–105, 145–147; core, 41–43, 66, 160; diversification of, 46, 146; ethnic studies in, 152; interdisciplinary, 152; new comprehensive, 143; package acceptance of, 160; state master plans for coordinating, 7

D

DARNES, B. R., 47

Delaware, 110–111, 164

DENNISON, J. D., 132

Disadvantaged students, 29, 84

District of Columbia, 111–112

Drop-back pattern, 2–3, 48

Dropouts, 3, 18

DUPUIS, P., 135

E

Educational Amendments Act, 24, 160–161

Educational-needs inventory, 113

Elective credit, 45, 48, 79, 89, 99; for experimental courses, 152; summary of, 151

Empire State College, 86

Equal opportunity for success, 28, 148

Esso Education Foundation, 7

Examination, 22; credit by, 18, 36, 42, 60, 64, 79, 82, 87, 152–153,

162; through CLEP, 79, 82, 152–153; criterion-based vs. norm-referenced, 158; degree-granting by, 87

Extension systems, 72

External degree programs, 152–153

F

Faculty: acceptance of policies by, 43; bargaining rights of, 102; Ed.D. program for, 154; as standard-setters, 97; state approval of, 61

Federal City College, 112

Federal influences, 160–161

Financial problems, 156

FINDIKYAN, N., 9

Flexibility in articulation, 150–156

Florida: admissions in, 38; articulation in, 10, 35–41, 150; associate degree in, 37–38, 150; baccalaureate in, 38; catalog as contract in, 38; Coordinating Commission in, 36, 38–40; experimental programs in, 39; general education agreement in 37; high school articulation in, 21, 40; introductory courses in, 38; research in, 40; statewide plan in, 33; summary of, 165; transfer information in, 149; upper-division institutions in, 148

Florida Atlantic University, 147

Foothill College, 2–3

Foreign language requirements, 101, 104

Forest Park Community College, 21

Formal articulation: in Florida, 35–41; in Georgia, 41–43; in Texas, 43–46

G

General education, 31, 103, 148; core of, 41–43. *See also* individual states

George Washington University, 112

Georgia: articulation in, 33, 41–43, 165; core curriculum in, 41–43

GLEAZER, E. J., JR., 11

Grades: as admissions requirements, 50, 62, 71, 73, 74, 80, 89–90, 152; D, 43, 55, 67, 73, 77–78, 80, 82, 90, 157; high school, role of, 54–

55; Knoell-Medsker study of, 7–8;
multidimensional, 161; nonpunitive, 156–158, 161; and performance evaluation, 111, 157, 162;
review of, 152, 156–157, 161; used
in gradepoint averages, 77
Graduate and upper-division institutions, 51, 72, 83, 88, 136, 147–148

H

Handbooks. *See* Publications on
transfer
HANSEN, J. S., 145
Hartnell College, 4
Hawaii: articulation in, 66–69; higher
education system in, 66, 68; summary of, 165; transfer of preprofessional credits in, 68
HENDERSON, L., 30
High school–community college articulation, 17–25; accrediting agency
role in, 23–24; advantage of, 18;
of career education, 24–25; in
Colorado, 110; counseling in, 19–
23; difficulty of, 18; in Florida, 21,
40; handbooks for, 19, 22; in New
York, 84–85; in Oregon, 63; programs for by state, 19–23; responsibility for, 19; university aid to,
23; of vocational/technical program, 23–24
High school students in community
colleges, 18–20, 40, 85
HILLS, J. R., 15
HOOVER, J. L., 11

I

Idaho, 112, 165
Illinois, 5; admissions guidelines in,
49–50; articulation in, 10, 33, 46–
51; enrollments in, 48; grading systems in, 157; institutional integrity
in, 150; master plan in, 46–48, 50;
problems remaining in, 50–51; reverse transfer in, 48; student consideration in, 48–49; summary of,
165
Independent study, 64, 79, 154–155
Indiana, 112–113, 166

Inquiry on New and Unsolved Transfer Problems, 150, 156
Institutional integrity, 150, 161
Institutional system–type articulation,
66–95; in Arizona, 73–76; in Hawaii, 66–69; in Iowa, 76–77; in
Kentucky, 69–70; in Massachusetts,
77–80; in Mississippi, 80–81; in
Nevada, 70–72; in New Jersey, 81–
83; in New York, 83–86; in Pennsylvania, 87–90; in Washington,
90–95
Instruction, officers for, 145
Iowa, 76–77, 166
Iowa, University of, 76, 147, 149

J

JENSEN, A. M., 145
JOHNSON, B. L., 11
Joint Committee on Junior and Se-
nior Colleges, 5, 6, 124
JONES, G., 132

K

Kansas, 7, 114–115, 166
Kentucky, 69–70, 166
KINTZER, F., 10, 16, 86, 145
KNOELL, D. M., 6–7, 10, 15–16, 124;
summary of study by, 8–9

L

LANGE, A. F., 12
Legally based articulation in Illinois,
46–51
LEWIS, I. G., 20
Los Angeles City College, 4, 25
Louisiana, 114, 166

M

Maine, 115, 166
Major field: core curriculum for, 44,
59; declaring, 44; requirements
for, 38, 44, 60; senior institution
control over, 28, 89
Manitoba, 132–133
Mars Hill College, 54, 56
Maryland, 7, 115, 167
Massachusetts, 77–79, 167
Massachusetts, University of, 78, 147

Massachusetts Institute of Technology, 151

Master plan, state: Arkansas, 109; California, 97; educational-needs studies for, 113; guidelines for, 10; Illinois, 46–48; Kansas, 113; Knoell-Medsker recommendations on, 7; Louisiana, 114; Montana, 116; Nevada, 70; New Jersey, 81; New York, 85; Oklahoma, 56; Pennsylvania, 87; South Dakota, 120; summary of, 123; Tennessee, 121; Texas, 43; Virginia, 64

MEDSKER, L. L., 4, 6–7, 10–11, 15–16, 124, 154; summary of study by, 8–9

Miami-Dade Junior College, 19

Michigan: agreement on two-year requirements in, 103–105; articulation in, 102–106; associate degree in, 103–104; curriculum articulation in, 105; institutional integrity in, 150; summary of, 167

Michigan, University of, 147, 149

Minnesota, 115, 167

Minnesota, University of, 151

Mississippi, 115–116, 167

Missouri, 21, 80, 168

Montana, 116, 168

MUIRHEAD, P. P., 24–25

N

National Association of Junior Colleges, 13

National Project for Improvement of Articulation Between Two-Year and Four-Year Colleges, 7, 9

Nebraska, 116–117, 168

NELSON, J. H., 6

Nevada, 70–72, 168

New England Association of Colleges and Secondary Schools, 24

New Hampshire, 117, 168

New Jersey: articulation in, 81–83; cluster plan in, 81; counseling in, 82; institutional integrity in, 150; summary of, 168; varying policies in, 82

New Mexico, 117, 169

New River Community College, 22–23

New York: adult education in, 85; agricultural-technical schools in, 83, 85; articulation in, 10, 83–87; cooperative college centers in, 84; external degree programs in, 153; full opportunity programs in, 84; high school–community college articulation in, 22, 84–85; problems remaining in, 85–86; regional plan for, 85–86; summary of, 169; urban centers in, 84–85

New York Institute of Technology, 151

Newman Report, 154–155

NICHOLSON, D. H., 53

NICKENS, J. M., 15

North Carolina: admissions policy in, 54–56; articulation in, 52–56; bachelor of technology degree in, 53, 151; problems remaining in, 56; summary of, 169; superboard in, 53; two-year institutions in, 53; vocation/technical programs in, 54, 151

North Dakota, 7, 117–118, 169

Northeastern University, 112

Northern Arizona University, 74

Nova University, 154

O

Occupational courses. See Vocational/technical courses

Ohio, 7, 118–119, 169

Oklahoma, 7; academic records in, 60; adult education in, 60; articulation in, 10, 33, 56–60; associate degrees in, 59, 150; baccalaureate in, 58–59; dual system in, 56; experimental programs in, 60; general education agreement in, 57–60, 150; introductory courses in, 59; problems remaining in, 60; summary of, 170; vocational schools in, 60

Ombudsman concept, 147, 160

Ontario, 133–134

Open-door policy, 18, 75, 100

Oregon: admissions in, 62; articulation in, 61–64; associate degree in, 62; secondary school articulation in, 63; state-approved curriculum in, 62; summary of, 170
Oregon State University, 63
Oregon Technical Institute, 63
Otero Junior College, 21

P

Package transfer plan, 94
Pass/fail grades, 156–157
Pennsylvania: articulation in, 87–90; bachelor of technology degree in, 89; goals of, 87–88; guides in, 88–89; master plan in, 87; private college policy in, 90; problems remaining in, 90; regional plan for, 88; summary of, 170
Pennsylvania State University, 88
Performance evaluation, 111, 157, 162
PLUSCH, J. O., 19
Portland Community College, 63
Princeton University, 82
Professional associations, 126
Professional education, 29, 146
Project TALENT, 16
Publications on transfer, 19, 22–23, 41, 46, 53, 64, 77, 82, 91, 103, 108, 110, 113; review of, 149

Q

Quebec, 134–139; admissions in, 138; classical colleges in, 135; community colleges in, 135–137; community participation in, 137; curriculum in, 138–139; governance in, 137; prerequisites problem in, 139; transfer in, 138–139; vocational program in, 135–137

R

Regional examining universities, 155
Residence requirements, 68, 71, 75
Reverse transfer, 2–3, 48
Rhode Island, 119–120, 170
Ricks College, 112
ROBSON, J. W., 13
Rutgers University, 82

S

SAKAGUCHI, M., 144
San Francisco Unified School District, 20
SANFORD, N., 157
Saskatchewan, 139–140
SCHERER, P. L., 10, 152–153
SCOPE research, 16
Seattle University, 91, 94
Senior institutions: admissions policy of, 8, 12, 27–29, 44, 49–50, 54–56, 59–60, 62, 65, 78, 97–98; barriers to articulation by, 27; complaints about community colleges by, 28; control over major field by, 89; discrimination against transfer students by, 8, 27, 90; enrollment lags in, 123; experimentation by, 39, 44, 60; inertia of, 9; normative exams by, 158; offices for articulation in, 146–147; prerogatives claimed by, 27–28, 90; probation and dismissal policies of, 8; publicizing requirements of, 59; recruitment of transfer students by, 124; school services of, 23, 102, 146–147; scrutiny of community college transcripts by, 27, 90–91
Shoreline Community College, 23
SIMONDS, H. E., 25
SMITH, A. K., 19
South Carolina, 120, 170
South Dakota, 120–121, 171
SPINDT, H. A., 12
Spokane Community College, 23
SPROUL, R. G., 13
SPURR, S. H., 158–159
State agencies, articulation by, 52–66, 144, 159; in North Carolina, 52–56; in Oklahoma, 56–61; in Oregon, 61–64; in Virginia, 64–66
STRONG, E. W., 13
Students, community college: academic work problems of, 8; characteristics of, 16; disadvantaged, 29, 84; dissatisfaction with four-year schools among, 3; emotional immaturity of, 3; failure of, 2–3;

flow of, 1; gifted, 18; lack of skills of, 2; mobility of, 9
Subject-area (discipline) articulation, 76, 81, 96, 147

T

Taft College, 3, 4
Technical courses. *See* Vocational/technical courses
Technical two-year institutions, 53–56, 72, 76, 83, 110–112, 120; in Canada, 128–129, 131, 133, 135–139
Tennessee, 121, 171
Testing of transfer students, 55, 65, 108
Test. *See* Examination
Texas, 5; articulation in, 43–46; core curriculum in, 43–46, 150; institutional integrity in, 150; principles of articulation in, 43–44; problems remaining in, 46; summary of, 171
Texas, University of, 149
Thomas Edison College, 153
THORNTON, J. W., JR., 11
TILLERY, D., 11, 16, 154
Transfer: from another state, 48; without associate degree, 66; attitudes toward, 2; automatic, 86, 111, 161; from career-oriented programs, 85, 151; flexibility in, 150–156; guaranteed, 36, 85–86; guidelines for, 9–10, 146; and high school grades, 54–55; information on, 149; limitations on, informing students of, 28, 45; package, 94; research on, 16; reverse, 2–3, 48; shock of, 14–15; tests before, 55, 65, 108. *See also* Articulation; Credit; Grades; individual states
Transfer (college-preparatory) programs: cooperative development of, 48, 56; experimental, 39, 44, 60, 152–156; individuality of, 14, 30; initiated by community colleges, 13–14, 26; purpose of, 30, 161; rigor of, 14; state approval of, 61; state-recommended, 62

Transfer students: accommodation of, 123, 126; appeals by, 126; characteristics of, 8, 16; discrimination against, 8, 27; equal access to upper division for, 14, 160; evaluation of, 7–8; financial problems of, 8; giving priority to, 79, 93, 98; guidelines for considering, 48–49; information possessed by, 4; Knoell-Medsker study of, 6, 8–9; mobility of, 9; ombudsman for, 147; orientation for, 4, 7, 27, 102; persistence of, 15; preparation for upper division of, 30, 161; residence requirements for, 68; self-confidence of, 2–4, 8; soliciting of, 124; studies of, 14–16, 83; success of, 7–8, 13–16, 27, 79; technical, 53–56; testing of, 55, 65, 108; versus "natives," 27, 79

U

Universities. *See* Senior institutions
Upper division related to lower division, 27, 30, 159, 161
Upper-division universities, 51, 72, 83, 88, 136, 147–148; in Florida, 148; status of, 148
Utah, 121–122, 171

V

Vermont, 122, 171
Veysey Bill, 19
Virginia: admissions in, 65; articulation in, 64–66; associate degree in, 65–66; general education in, 66; guidelines in, 64; institutional integrity in, 150; summary of, 172
Vocational/technical courses: adding new, 146; in armed services, 151; barriers against, 27; in California, 97; elective credit for, 151; by industry, 151; in Iowa, 76; mandatory, 76; in Pennsylvania, 89; in Quebec, 135; summary of transfer of, 151; in Wisconsin, 72–73; women in, 137. *See also* individual states

Voluntary-type articulation, 43, 96–123, 160
VROMAN, C., 5

W

WARREN, J. R., 157
Washington: articulation in, 90–95; associate degree in, 91–95; communication in, 91; guidelines in, 92; institutional integrity in, 150; package transfer in, 94; summary of, 172
Washington, University of, 91, 94, 147, 149, 151
Washington State University, 91, 94–95
WATTENBARGER, J. L., 5, 7, 8, 18, 21, 28, 29, 144; articulation model of, 124–125, 160
Wenatchee Valley College, 23

West Florida, University of, 148
West Virginia, 122–123, 172
Western Carolina University, 54
Western Washington State College, 9, 94, 147
WILLINGHAM, W. W., 9, 10
WILSON, G. C., 29
Wisconsin: articulation in, 72–73; center system in, 72; credit for vocational courses in, 151; extension system in, 72; summary of, 172; technical institutes in, 72–73
Work experience, credit for, 64, 152, 155
Working rules for transfer credit, 152
Wyoming, 123, 172

Y

Yakima Valley College, 23

LB2328.K44
Kintzer, Middleman in higher education [

3 1510 00055 3660